The Internet Entrepreneurs

books for the future minded

Welcome to the next generation of business.

There is a new world which we can look at but we cannot see. Yet within it, the forces of technology and imagination are overturning the way we work and the way we do business.

ft.com books are both gateway and guide to this world. We understand it because we are part of it. But we also understand the needs of businesses which are taking their first steps into it, and those still standing hesitantly on the threshold. Above all, we understand that, as with all business challenges, the key to success lies not with the technology itself, but with the people who must use it and manage it.

People like you – the future minded.

See a world of business.

Visit **www.ft.com** today.

The Internet Entrepreneurs

Business rules are good: break them

Christopher Price

**books for the
future minded** *An imprint of* **Pearson Education**

London • New York • San Francisco • Toronto • Sydney • Tokyo • Singapore
Hong Kong • Cape Town • Madrid • Amsterdam • Munich • Paris • Milan

PEARSON EDUCATION LIMITED

Head Office
Edinburgh Gate
Harlow CM20 2JE
Tel: +44 (0)1279 623623
Fax: +44 (0)1279 431059

London Office:
128 Long Acre
London WC2E 9AN
Tel: +44 (0)20 7447 2000
Fax: +44 (0)20 7240 5771
www.business-minds.com

First published in Great Britain in 2000

ISBN 0 273 64921 3

British Library Cataloguing in Publication Data
A CIP catalogue record for this book can be obtained from the British Library.

10 9 8 7 6 5 4 3 2 1

Designed by Sue Lamble Graphic Design
Typeset by Pantek Arts Ltd, Maidstone, Kent
Printed and bound in Great Britain by Biddles Ltd, Guildford & King's Lynn

The Publishers' policy is to use paper manufactured from sustainable forests.

To Alison

About the author

Until March 2000, Christopher Price was the information technology correspondent of the *Financial Times*. Prior to that, he held a variety of editorial posts over a ten-year period at the *FT*, including financial reporter, where he specialised in the media and communications industries. He is currently editor of EOnews.net, a financial services website. *The Internet Entrepreneurs* is his first book. He lives and works in London.

Contents

Acknowledgments / xiii

Introduction / xv

1 Bob Davis Lycos
Searching out the next deal / 1

Introduction / 3
Joining Lycos / 5
The Lycos business strategy / 8
The Lycos acquisition strategy / 10
The Lycos partnership strategy / 12
USA Networks merger – what went wrong? / 14

2 Jerry Yang Yahoo!
Size matters / 19

Introduction / 21
The formation of Yahoo! / 22
The Yahoo! business strategy / 24
Yahoo!'s working culture / 30
The Yahoo! partnership strategy / 31

3 Jay Walker Priceline
Storming the barricades of commerce / 35

Introduction / 37
The formation of Priceline / 38
The Priceline concept / 41
The Delta deal / 44
Latest initiatives / 46

4 Jim Barksdale Netscape
Proof that adult supervision works / 51

Introduction / 53
Joining Netscape / 54
Rapid growth for Netscape / 57
America Online (AOL) acquires Netscape / 61
What next for Jim Barksdale? / 62

5 Jeff Bezos Amazon
Building the net's biggest brand / 65

Introduction / 67
The formation of Amazon / 68
Latest initiatives / 71
Plans for future expansion / 75

6 Christos Cotsakos E*Trade
Courage under fire / 79

Introduction / 81
Christos Cotsakos – a personal history / 82
*Joining E*Trade / 88*
Difficult early days / 91
Plans for the future / 93

7 David Hayden Critical Path
Innovation as a way of life / 97

Introduction / 99
The formation of Critical Path / 100
Initial challenges / 106
*E*Trade signs up / 107*
Hayden today / 109

8 Steve Kirsch Infoseek
Altruism born of technology talent / 113

Introduction / 115
The formation of Infoseek / 117
Future plans for Kirsch / 121

9 **Rod Schrock** AltaVista
From big business to net start-up / 127

Introduction / 129
Joining AltaVista / 131
Schrock's business strategy for AltaVista / 134
Possible future partnerships / 138

10 **Joe Kraus** Excite
Passion and commitment to a business ideal / 143

Introduction / 145
The formation of Excite / 145
Kraus's particular role at Excite / 150
Funding the 'big idea' / 152
George Bell becomes CEO / 155
Necessary changes for the future / 157

11 **Candice Carpenter** and **Nancy Evans** iVillage
A different vision of net success / 161

Introduction / 163
How iVillage evolved / 164
iVillage's working culture / 167
Future developments / 170

12 **Pierre Omidyar** eBay
Bidding to distance the competition / 177

Introduction / 179
The formation of eBay / 179
Rapid growth for eBay / 182
Challenges and potential problems / 185
Looking to the future / 189

Index / 191

Acknowledgments

I would like to thank the following people for their help with this book: Richard Stagg of Pearson Education, whose enthusiasm helped stimulate the project and whose encouragement supported it through its many gestations. Louise Kehoe and Paul Taylor, who have been so generous in sharing their extensive experience and knowledge of all things IT. Jaine Gunn, who patiently and cheerfully transcribed numerous tapes. Alan Cane for frequent moments of insight. Rebecca Hartley at Siemens UK for the Scenic laptop that much of this book was written on. John Ridding, managing editor of the *FT*, for enabling me to take the time for research and writing.

Introduction

It takes guts to lose money

Particularly when it's other people's and especially when it adds up to $4 billion.

That is roughly the sum the 13 internet entrepreneurs featured in this book lost in 1999. To be fair, a couple of them, like Yahoo's Jerry Yang, have moved into the black, or, like Netscape's Jim Barksdale, have stepped away from running a business in favour of investing.

But the point is that all 13 have in the past – and in the main have continued to do so – racked up hundreds of millions of dollars in losses with no end in sight.

Doesn't all that red ink irk their entrepreneurial sensibilities? Indeed it does, which is why it takes enormous bravery to keep on course when the business is hemorrhaging cash, when your investors need constant reassuring, when the workforce craves inspiration and when venture capitalists demand nearly all your equity.

The pain is possibly eased from the knowledge that despite these hefty losses, the 12 companies had a combined market capitalization of $170 billion, giving the 13 entrepreneurs a combined wealth of more than $35 billion.

It was not just bravery, however, that qualified the business people chosen for this book. The purpose was to gather a wide variety of the leading managers in the internet industry and quiz them about their strategies, their motivations and their ambitions at this crucial point in the evolution of the new medium.

This would then build up a picture of influences, experiences and beliefs that could point to what it is that makes these leaders of the internet revolution so special, what it is that marks them out. In short, just how they have broken the rules.

Jeff Bezos of Amazon appears by virtue of his enormous reputation in the e-commerce market. The internet's biggest retail brand is also the template for a myriad other web businesses. Bezos's views, often controversial, spell out the future for Amazon, and consequently point the way for many other internet ventures.

Bob Davis of Lycos heads one of the biggest search engine groups. Managing the migration of the advertising-driven business to one in which e-commerce will play a greater role is a significant challenge and one that will be followed closely by others in the same space.

Candice Carpenter and Nancy Evans of iVillage are the only women entrepreneurs featured. However, this is not their only claim for inclusion – they are also the only internet community site to feature, and as such face unique challenges in monetizing their business.

Jerry Yang of Yahoo! leads perhaps the strongest brand on the web. The original folk hero of the internet, Yahoo has been the most successful search engine group and continues to be the company that its rivals strive to catch. Yang's strategy, designed to take Yahoo to the next stage of its development, will be crucial to maintaining its lead.

Rod Schrock of AltaVista appears, at first glance, perhaps to be an odd choice for inclusion. A veteran of the computer industry, he was brought into the search engine group relatively recently to rejuvenate its strategy. However, one of the fascinating aspects of the internet is its sheer pace of change, and Schrock's managerial spurs hinge on his ability to move quickly.

Pierre Omidyar of eBay founded one of the web's most famous success stories. His auction site has unleashed an enormous business opportunity, one which dozens if not hundreds of others have sought to copy. However, eBay remains the clear market leader – and Omidyar is determined to keep it that way.

Jay Walker of Priceline is religious in his conviction that his business holds the future for retailing the world over. His name-your-price business model has created enormous ructions, first in the airline industry, and lately in the car rental market. His beliefs in the future of web commerce could hold the key to restructuring across a range of industries.

Christos Cotsakos of E*Trade threw up a secure job in the old world economy to take the reins of one of the companies that has revolutionized the US financial services industry. While the bricks and mortar companies are hitting back, the decorated Vietnam veteran is adamant that they will not deflect E*Trade from its path.

Joe Kraus of Excite@Home helped build one of the best-known names on the web. The search engine group has opted to become part of the @Home group in its belief that bandwidth holds the future for many in the portal space. Kraus's views reveal a company at the crossroads.

Jim Barksdale of Netscape has become an industry legend. He reveals he turned down Bill Gates's offer of a senior post at Microsoft to take up the post at the internet browser group. Now a venture capitalist, Barksdale lists what it takes to attract his funding in a net start-up.

David Hayden of Critical Path appears because of his roller-coaster internet career, which started with the family of Robert Maxwell, the disgraced British media baron, and continues now with his new venture and his plans for a VC fund unlike any other.

Steve Kirsch of Infoseek could be seen as the odd one out of all our entrepreneurs. The search engine group was sold to Disney in the hope that the combined entity would score better than alone. However, the jury remains out and Kirsch is setting out on his own again in a technology-driven venture.

Thirteen people who have made an indelible mark on the internet. How they did so is revealed in the next 12 chapters. But out of them we can draw several conclusions – ways in which the entrepreneurs took accepted business logic and twisted, bent and in some cases broke the rules.

Breaking the rules

1 Do not be afraid to lose money

What's $4 billion when market analysts forecast that the internet economy will be worth $3.3 trillion in 2003? It's a question well worth asking: if your company is first to market in a business revolution, what price success?

Building market share, establishing a brand and buying customers are all common parlance to internet companies. How much one pays to get there and how long it takes to achieve some sort of critical mass are the $4 billion questions.

Which is where holding one's nerve in the face of mounting losses, with the knowledge that the future is uncertain, that pay-day may never come, and if it does then not in the way your business plan forecast, comes in.

And at the same time, the cynics and critics, of which there are many, carp about the internet bubble about to burst, about overvalued stock prices, about unsustainable business models and the overhyped individuals at the industry's heart.

Losing money hurts. It goes against every capitalist's grain. Yet for the foresighted and far-sighted it is a risk worth taking to seize the high ground and to gain control.

It is not that we have not been here before either. Take the example of other so-called blue sky investments – mobile phone and television cable companies.

industry's explosive growth at the end of the 1990s. But in 1997 the idea of handing over your most sensitive communications to a third party was seen as plain ridiculous.

Yet Hayden too was blessed with a tenacity common to our 13 entrepreneurs. His tale ends with him heading a multi-billion dollar business and arguing the tribulations of technology with President Bill Clinton. The journey in between is engrossing.

3 The best ideas are original – and scalable

Don't think niche. Niche is for wimps. An original idea should be just that: fresh, innovative and inventive. Most of all, it should be scalable. It should be able to grow to its ultimate potential. It comes back to marketing, to development expenditure, to managerial resources. They should all be in place – and ready to be increased if the situation requires it. Being first, building a brand, are crucial for web success.

Nothing demonstrates this better than the case of Netscape. Jim Barksdale tells how he tore up the accountancy rule book in order for the fast-growing company to expand at an even greater rate.

So too Jeff Bezos at Amazon. Building a bookstore on the web was an original thought. But throwing the huge amount of resources at the venture that Bezos did was deemed crazy by many analysts. Four years later, and the US part of the book business turned profitable in the fourth quarter of 1999.

Not that that has made Bezos smug. Far from it. He has taken the Amazon concept of great customer service and low prices to other areas of commerce. The scale of his enterprise appears limitless.

Finally, consider how eBay broke the mould. The first mass market auction site was not only a first rate idea, but also limitless in its potential. Yet Pierre Omidyar, eBay's founder, could have positioned the company as simply a regional player. That he chose not to is testament to his ambition and self-belief in the concept of the company.

proposition than say five years ago. Today's VCs see giving advice and nurturing their investments as a primary requirement.

However, it was not always the case, and still is not in less developed capital markets outside of Silicon Valley. Supportive investors will count when it matters most – when the 'burn rate' in one's venture has to be ramped up, when new partnerships are being sought and when targets are proving hard to achieve.

Take Joe Kraus, and the other founders of Excite, one of the internet's biggest search engine groups, and bigger still since its acquisition by @Home.

It's 1994, and with the internet in its infancy, these six Stanford college kids develop an innovative piece of software that searches and sorts through the world wide web. They admit to potential backers that they have no idea how to make money from this, but if someone is willing to help them develop that side of the business too, then all well and good.

The response is underwhelming. Nothing. A big zero. The notion of incubating some smart kids with management expertise is unheard of, even in Silicon Valley.

But the Excite founders stick with it. They continue to turn up for meetings with venture capitalists in shorts and T-shirts. They carry on harassing bankers and potential backers.

In short, they continue to believe not only in the power of their product and the potential of the business, but also the value of their team. That is and was brave. Discovering just how they managed to convince an investor to take a chance and jump in makes even more fascinating reading.

Then there is David Hayden. Down on his luck after getting divorced and having to sell his first internet business too cheaply, he casts around for a new venture. And it's this: managing the e-mail for big businesses.

This is just the sort of notion that we might take for granted today – after all outsourcing has been the bedrock of much of the technology

4 Put the customer at the centre of the business

Behind every successful dotcom is a happy customer base. Research has shown that net users are far more likely to shun a website after a bad experience than in the bricks and mortar world. Poor customer service, it seems, is a big click-off.

At the same time, the traffic rates for sites with great service multiply dramatically due to the internet's viral nature.

Jerry Yang recalls how Yahoo was faced with the dilemma of which direction to take the company – either to a paid-for service, or an advertising-driven free service.

They chose the latter and the decision could have been suicidal: why would net users visit a free website? Surely, like newspapers and magazines, such a concept would be equated with low-brow, downmarket, inferior goods?

Not so. Yahoo served up a free service second to none in which they put the Yahoo customer at the centre. All the new services that were to be added would be user-driven – most powerfully with the introduction of the 'MyYahoo' concept, enabling users to personalize the service.

5 Play to your strengths – spread control

Control is a natural emotion that needs to be kept under control. No manager can hope to oversee every aspect of a business, particularly one that is destined to grow rapidly.

A recurring theme from the 13 entrepreneurs is how good they have been, and remain, about delegating responsibilities. They play to their strengths – as team leaders, as motivators, as innovators, whatever. But they do not pretend to be the best operational executives, or the smartest technologists.

This aspect has become a dominant theme at iVillage, where managers stick to what they are good at, a move that Candice Carpenter reckons has increased the company's efficiency significantly.

Another good example is Excite. Joe Kraus says that he and the other founders were adamant that for the company to expand in the way they envisaged, they would need 'adult supervision'. In short, they wanted an experienced manager to take the reins.

Likewise, who could fault Pierre Omidyar's decision to bring in Meg Whitman to run the operations at eBay? Omidyar admits to being an ideas man, and strategy continues to be his strength.

Jerry Yang describes himself as 'Chief Yahoo', a title that gives him a roving brief, enabling the co-founder to touch upon every part of the company's operations. It is, he says, his way of keeping the Yahoo spirit burning brightly throughout the organization.

Five ways our internet entrepreneurs differentiated themselves from the myriad other dotcom ventures. But over the next 12 chapters, you will also discover where they got their early business influences from, what drove them to their destiny and what motivates them to continue.

Detailed analysis of how each executive did things differently – and what challenges remain – are laid out. It combines into a story that peels away the mystique of the internet market, and reveals the type of business psyche behind some of the world's most successful internet entrepreneurs.

One of the things I believe in here very, very strongly is that if you let up you lose.

Bob Davis
Lycos

Searching out the next deal

I'm a jack of all trades and a master of none. I'm clearly involved in a strategic role looking at mergers and acquisitions issues, but I'm also one of the company's passionate Q&A specialists, forever conducting product reviews, assessing users' experience, addressing quality issues with the product teams here.

I'm not trying to micromanage the business, but I am trying to instill a sense of fanaticism as it relates to exceptional user experience. One of the things I believe in here very, very strongly is that if you let up you lose. That's what the sign says outside my door: you let up you lose.

Our mission here at Lycos is to become the most visited network and for that we must win people's time. We try to instill in everyone here that people have a choice – they do not have to use Lycos. There are 600 million pages, 600 million choices to go to when you log onto the internet. I have to recognize that there's always a contest. I have to earn you as a user of Lycos services. We earn that through a great user experience, not an acceptable one, or a grade one one, but a great one. So that's my focus: looking at the products, making sure they're good, developing and doing what they need.

Introduction

For a man who prides himself on his negotiating skills, losing an $18 billion deal must hurt. Yet if Bob Davis is still smarting over the collapse, in early 1999, of the merger between Lycos, the internet company he heads, and the USA Networks home shopping business, he hides it well.

The deal would have brought together the internet's second biggest media portal and America's largest television home shopping audience. Such a marriage between new and old media worlds was the stuff of every convergent theorist's dreams, bringing e-commerce to the unconverted and giving on-line shoppers the delivery systems and secure payment facilities they yearn for. And for Davis, the merger, in which Lycos was to be subsumed by Barry Diller's USA Networks, would have been the culmination of a flurry of deals that had helped propel Lycos from the fifth most visited internet site to second in little more than a year.

At the time of the agreement, in February 1999, Davis said: 'With one fell swoop we have created the framework to becoming the largest e-commerce entity anywhere, ever.' Diller, who would have been chairman to Davis's chief executive in the new USA Lycos Interactive Networks, said prophetically: 'I think we are at a period of new convergence, and the new convergence is about information, entertainment and direct selling.'

Davis now admits to a 'misjudgement' over how the affair was handled. He says Lycos shareholders, whose hostility to the deal eventually sank it, 'misunderstood' the valuation concept. But unbowed, he adds, 'When you're a pioneer sometimes you claim new territory and sometimes you take some arrows.' He pauses, 'We took some arrows.'

These 'arrows' included a rash of lawsuits from angry shareholders, alleging they had been misled by management over the timing of the deal, criticism from Wall Street that the deal badly undervalued the search engine group, and concern also that the three-month affair had distracted senior management.

For a consummate deal-maker like Davis, a man renowned for his energy, tenacity and above all his vision, the affair raised questions about his judgement. Indeed, many observers were surprised the chief executive survived the costly episode unscathed.

However, Davis had no doubts about his position: 'I didn't feel remotely vulnerable. Lots of people misjudged the market.'

Did he consider resigning?

'Not for a moment. Remember, I built this company up from nothing – why would I want to resign?'

Perhaps because he felt let down by his major shareholders?

'Not true. We have very strong relations with all our big investors. Just look at our shareholder register – we have the same investors now as we did prior to the USA deal.'

Davis has since resumed where he left off prior to the USA affair, building the Lycos Network, forging alliances, making acquisitions and extending the Lycos reach to ever-greater audiences. In April 1999, he was rewarded

>> Prior to the USA Networks deal, all that
                Davis touched turned to internet gold

with the news that the company had beaten archrival Yahoo for the first time in terms of audience reach. It has since slipped behind again, but the press cutting from the *Boston Globe* heralding the great event hangs, ballooned up to giant size, in the lobby of Lycos's headquarters in Waltham, Massachusetts.

Joining Lycos

That he did rally from the USA setback owes much to Davis the entrepreneur, as well as the vagaries of the internet world.

Prior to the USA Networks deal, all that Davis touched turned to internet gold. In a series of canny acquisitions and smart alliances, he transformed Lycos from being just another search engine group into one of the web's most valuable properties.

It was done through a vision of the internet as simply another medium through which to attract the largest possible audience and extract the maximum commercial returns. And by cleverly guessing what visitors to the internet wanted – interaction, community and service – Davis was able to acquire businesses to serve these needs at a fraction of the cost his competitors would later pay.

Even more impressively, this was all started by a man who had never used the internet before, by a company late to the game, and based away from the hotbed of technology in Silicon Valley in less than salubrious Waltham. It was perhaps apt therefore that, while Davis's internet peers had either a technology or media background, his was in sales.

The call to join the new Lycos internet venture came, in 1995, from Dan Nova at Highland Capital, a venture capital group. It had licensed the technology behind Lycos from Carnegie Mellon University, where technicians had invented the 'spider' search engine the previous year – *Lycos* is the Latin name for 'wolf spider.'

Davis recalls: 'My experience of the internet was not just minimal, it was non-existent.' This was despite his working in high-technology environments, first for Wang, the computer manufacturer, and then for Cambex, a computer storage company.

'I had known Dan at Wang, before he left to become a venture capitalist ten or so years ago,' says Davis. 'He'd come across the spider at this university – and a scientist who had no interest in commercializing it.' He adds somewhat bemused, 'He just wanted to be a researcher all his life.'

5 ways...

Bob Davis
broke the
rules

1 Left the security of his job to become the first employee of a company based solely on a piece of technology he knew hardly anything about.

2 Imposed a standard media model on Lycos and developed its unique multi-brand strategy.

3 Spotted the portal potential early and paid less and bought more smartly than his rivals.

4 Bold enough to walk away from the USA Shopping Networks deal.

5 Developed the Lycos brand worldwide by giving away equity to foreign partners.

One of the things that interested Davis immediately was the concept of a venture capital firm licensing something like this: 'That was pretty unusual in that VCs typically invest in people and business plans – they very rarely invest in technology.'

Nova first contacted Davis in early 1995:

'Dan called me up one day and asked what I knew about the internet. I said: "Absolutely nothing." He said: "Well let's forget about that question."

'Then we spoke for a little while, then we spoke for a long time. I got to look at it seriously, and though I hadn't been a web user, I was beginning to get wrapped up in it. I believed we had a new phenomenon in the making, although I can't say I was entirely convinced. Fortunately, I made the right decision to join.'

The opportunity to start his own business had also been stirring in Davis:

'I'd always thought of myself as an entrepreneur-in-waiting in the sense that I'd always wanted to start and run my own business.

'For any number of reasons the opportunities had never presented them-selves, or I had never had the fortitude to go ahead and do it. But it was always a strong burning desire.'

He traces his business roots back to the age of ten when he recalls selling newspapers on the street corner. This quickly progressed to mail order catalogues, in which the teenage Bob Davis would act as the agent, selling anything from seeds to wrapping paper.

But there was another key driver in his early development: the death of his parents around this time. This underpinned what he admits was a 'very competitive' attitude, particularly evident in sports competitions, and underlining his desire to win.

Because of his circumstances, he was also very independent and developed a great sense of self-reliance. He recalls:

'I had to put myself through school, I had no other choice. And while we were not exactly poor, we were certainly a working class family.

'So there was probably quite a lot of that in there, helping me to aspire to compete and do a little better. When you're left there by yourself, your psyche develops in that way.'

His time as a salesman, at Wang as director of worldwide marketing and then as vice-president of sales at Cambex, he sees as well spent. But when the approach came, he was ready:

'The fact that I was established, that I had enough of a nest egg, that I felt I could protect my family and my assets in the event that this thing went wrong, was important.

'So I was ready at this point to go out and take a gamble. I left a great job behind, things were positioning very well, my career was blossoming – and I left to become the only employee of this thing no one had ever heard of!'

Davis, a large-framed man with a spring of nervous energy, laughs at the memory of what must have been the most terrifying moment for any entrepreneur. 'I remember telling friends that I was going off to work for this internet company and they said: "What? Are you crazy?!"'

It was June 1995 and Davis was 39. His first assignment as Lycos's only employee was to negotiate the terms of the licensing agreement with the university. Given that the internet was in its infancy and that no one had much of a concept about its potential, it was to prove a good training ground for much of what was to come for Davis.

He had written a business plan for Lycos prior to taking up his appointment:

'It was partly for my own benefit, principally trying to understand what this thing could be.

'And I saw a couple of opportunities as to how this might shape – one of which was a software model, and the other one a media model. We, of course, opted for the media model and that's done well for us, but there are still software components as we continue to license technologies and services of an albeit smaller part of our business.'

The Lycos business strategy

The Lycos business strategy has been a major exercise in brand building. Significantly, the company has not attempted to subsume any of the companies it has acquired. Rather it has sought to build the brands within the 'Lycos Network', while at the same time cut costs through the centralization of much of the sales and marketing functions.

'The Network is modeled after the proven branding models used by every major media company in the world,' says Davis, writing in the last company annual report. 'Simply put, we divide our audience by viewer interest or demographics into one of many properties – each with its own brand and personality. The properties are then aggregated into the Network to take advantage of sales and overhead efficiencies.'

Davis believes that this multi-branding strategy is the key differentiator between Lycos and the other media portals – and one which will give it the best returns in the long run. He tells me:

'Right from the beginning, we wrapped ourselves around the idea of a multi-brand network. We believed, and have been proved right, that this is the way to establish a thriving, developing and ongoing media property.

'So, while we have continued to build the Lycos brand, side by side we have launched a large number of other sites and destinations, either through organic growth or through acquisitions.'

>> Davis believes that this multi-branding strategy is the key differentiator between Lycos and the other media portals

Not everyone has been convinced by a strategy that has the potential to distract attention away from a company's main brand and on to smaller less valuable properties. 'At the time, I think most folk looked at us with a degree of puzzlement,' admits Davis.

'How do you build a web company across so many different brands? The answer is quite simple in that any media company of any scale that has ever existed has built itself across multiple brands.

'The same I believed was going to be true on the web, and in fact that has materialized. Today we own four of the top 20 web brands in existence, the Lycos Network reaches 47 percent of all web users, we have the largest community of users in the world, we are the fastest growing on-line network, we are a global media company operating in 24 countries and will add another six shortly.'

The list is reeled off by someone who sounds like they have had to pull out a lot of arrows, to demonstrate the giant steps Lycos has taken and to underline its determination to pursue its multi-brand and highly acquisitive strategy.

Davis is also at pains to point out that it is not simply a case of buying businesses to fit into a preordained plan; it is also about integrating them: 'A lot of companies have tried to make it happen. But many were wrapped in a state of confusion, not necessarily committed to either a multi- or uni-brand strategy – with the end result that you have something halfway in between and it goes nowhere.'

The Lycos way was different: 'Our plan was very, very simple. As we acquired these businesses we said they would no longer be run as independent stand-alone entities, simply because we had common elements across the Network: sales, human resources, finance, etc.'

Because these common elements could all be aggregated, this left the product teams to focus on developing their own areas of specialization. 'We operate business units, but not separate businesses,' says Davis. He explains further:

'It allowed us to take costs out of these businesses and enabled us to remove distractions away from the people who had built these products so well.

'The revenue generation from many of the great innovators wasn't something that came naturally, nor something that necessarily came with experience. So by pulling these things, like sales and marketing, away from them, we could allow them to carry on with product development better.'

The Lycos acquisition strategy

Acquisitions may have expanded the Lycos network substantially in the past three years, but it is the knitting together of the different businesses that has been at the root of the company's success. 'Integrating acquisitions is nothing short of a religion here,' says its chief executive proudly.

The cross-pollination and cross-fertilization from different parts of the Lycos Network has driven traffic from one site to another, reinforcing the overall brand and creating multiple opportunities for e-commerce and other revenue-generating ideas. Indeed driving traffic to another part of

1 Differentiating the Lycos service.

2 Make a bold acquisition – AltaVista for example – to catapult Lycos into the top portal tier.

3 Continue to build the Lycos brand, perhaps into other media.

4 Focus on what it does best: community, e-commerce and search.

5 Don't be put off by the collapse of the Shopping Networks deal. Do consider (again) partnering with a big media group.

5 hurdles...

for Bob Davis and Lycos

the Lycos Network is a key criterion used to measure individual managers' performance. 'Attracting an audience to one's own site is not good enough', says Davis emphatically. He continues:

'We don't find the brands competing against each other. On the contrary, we find them co-operating with one another. The reason brands exist in a normal media world is so that we can divide the audience either by interest or demographics, and a publisher hopes to create more revenues by doing that.'

>> Lycos has gained significant benefits from partnerships

Lycos's acquisition strategy has been driven by two criteria: a belief in a multi-faceted web experience for the user, and fear that its late start would quickly price the company out of the market. 'Our competitors were around up to a year before we were, and of course that's an eternity on the web,' says Davis. 'We were also significantly less funded than our competitors. Our capitalization prior to going public was just $2 million, and out of that we had to pay $750,000 to the university. That made our working capital $1.25 million available for the company. It's laughable by today's standards.'

But Lycos's IPO in 1997 enabled it to issue stock and launch its aggressive buying spree. It caused astonishment outside the internet market in

February 1998 when it paid $61 million for Tripod, a rapidly growing but still small internet community site. Tripod's value, as far as Lycos was concerned, was its software that enabled community members to build their own web pages – a common enough feature today but at the beginning of 1998 seen as a significant technological advantage. Despite the surprise at the price, it was soon seen as a harbinger of things to come; barely a year later Yahoo, Lycos's chief rival, paid $3.9 billion for Tripod's archcompetitor GeoCities.

Lycos's page-building technology was further enhanced with the acquisition of Angelfire, later in 1998. Other purchases have included:

- WhoWhere, a directory service for finding people on the internet
- MailCity, an e-mail facilitator
- HotBot, an advanced search engine
- MyTime.com, an on-line calendar service
- Wired News, a technology news and member site
- Gamesville.com, an interactive games portal
- Sonique, a music site.

The Lycos partnership strategy

Allied to its acquisition policy, like other media portals, Lycos has gained significant benefits from partnerships. These have been with both content companies and distribution groups. Recent examples of this include an agreement with IBM's Lotus, which will see the Lycos portal embedded in Lotus Notes Release 5, which could put the Black Retriever motif on some 38 million desktop PCs.

Extending the agreement further, IBM has agreed to place the Lycos start page on all new Aptiva PCs and ThinkPad mobile PCs. Packard Bell will also start to feature Lycos as its exclusive internet portal on its consumer PCs.

Other recent examples include a deal with America Online to feature the latter's instant messaging system, while Fidelity Investments will distribute Lycos products to their on-line investor community.

New e-commerce initiatives include a $52 million deal with WebMD, allowing the healthcare portal to be the sole supplier of medical products and services on the Lycos Network. A further $135 million could be generated for Lycos by a deal to allow Wingspan.com to sell financial services to Lycos members.

This all makes for a rosier bottom line. However, other recent initiatives smack too much of trying to catch up with nimbler competitors. An auction channel, an educational zone, and a shopping facilitator are all being delivered under the strategy of enriching the user experience – but hardly differentiate the network.

That said, Davis emphasizes the importance of the shopping initiative in particular. LYCOshop will enable small and medium-sized retailers to set up shop on the web; they get the Lycos Network traffic, the company takes its slice of the transactions. Sounds simple enough, but is little different to half a dozen similar ventures already under way, such as Amazon's z-shops.

However, Davis and Lycos have shown they have not lost their touch for success with their ambitions for Lycos's international expansion. The company has chosen to partner significant media or technology groups in their home markets, supplying technology and brand value in return for local content, management and operational services.

Lycos Europe is a joint venture with Bertlesmann, the private German media giant. It went public in March 2000 with a market valuation of more than $5 billion. It operates own-language services in six European countries, with as many again planned during 2000. As Davis proudly points out, Lycos's capital investment in the joint venture is zero.

There are similar operations in Japan, Korea and a south-east Asian site based in Singapore, all of which are likely to become public companies eventually and potentially put billions of dollars of assets on Lycos's balance sheet. Unlike its competitors, the company does not consolidate its overseas operations.

More recently, Lycos has announced plans to move into Russia and Latin America, and also expand its presence in Asia, all in partnership with local content providers.

USA Networks merger – what went wrong?

The right deals, smart acquisitions, savvy branding – that was the reputation Davis had built for Lycos by the beginning of 1999. It all makes the USA Networks episode all the more fascinating.

On paper, the merger made some sense. USA Networks had the 'old world' attributes of a 10 million television audience used to shopping over the phone, a 20 million credit card base with its Ticketmaster service, a call center able to handle 100 million inquiries a year, and a large distribution network. Add in the 30 million visitors to Lycos, and to Davis and Diller the cross-fertilization benefits were obvious. It appeared a match made in heaven.

Except the context was a little more complex than that. USA's foray into on-line commerce had been disappointing. Its Internet Shopping Network and First Auction businesses had not performed well against their contemporaries. Indeed the former business does not make the top 500 most visited websites in the Media Matrix rankings.

Furthermore, ISN was early to the game, commencing business in 1994. By the end of 1997, fourth quarter sales were just $ 6.7 million, tiny in both e-commerce terms and in its contribution to USA's overall business. At the same time, ISN's operating losses were rocketing, growing three times faster than revenue growth, a key valuation determinant on Wall Street. So much for cross-fertilization, cynics cried.

Sceptics also questioned whether a fast-growing net-savvy company like Lycos should be attaching itself to a slow-moving old media company such as USA Networks. Home Shopping Network's revenue rose just 7 percent in 1998, with operating income flat. Revenues at Ticketmaster increased just 3 percent, while its operating income actually declined.

It was these concerns, coupled with the lower than expected premium being put on Lycos's stock, that made some investors baulk. As the Lycos share price eroded, the company's biggest shareholder and founder, CMGI, withdrew its support for a deal it had previously agreed to in principle.

As Davis fought for the deal, meeting large investors and Wall Street analysts, Lycos was hit by a flurry of shareholder lawsuits which alleged that the management had misled investors over the USA deal. In particular, they were angered by remarks made by some directors relating to the future independence of the company just weeks before unveiling the agreement, a move which sent the share price tumbling.

Ironically, Davis's position was strengthened by his decision to walk away from the deal he had staked so much credibility on. Investor and analyst response was to applaud the brave move and the stock price subsequently recovered.

However, Davis's post was also secured by the continued support of CMGI – although reports that the affair has soured relations between Davis and CMGI boss David Wetherall cannot be quantified. Davis says he maintains a good working relationship with his biggest investor, but refuses to comment on a *Wall Street Journal* report the week before our meeting in mid-December 1999 that suggested CMGI was negotiating to buy Lycos. Neither would he be drawn on speculation that AltaVista, another CMGI company, might be pulled into a merger with Lycos. 'I think that's an unlikely scenario. If CMGI wanted to sell AltaVista to us, I guess we would be interested, but I don't think they do.'

Davis does not expect to be attracted by a deal similar to the USA Networks one in the near future – but believes that kind of transaction will become commonplace in the longer term: 'The deal represented a good opportunity for this company. But we clearly misjudged the market reaction to that. It was a pioneering transaction in that it attempted to merge offline and online assets and it created a difficult to understand valuation proposition. And we misjudged that piece of it.'

Not that Davis appears humbled by the experience:

'I think we've laid the ground for others – Abacus and Double Click, eBay and Butterfield & Butterfield, are two examples.

'As the market evolves they'll still be abundant opportunities because there aren't many internet leaders – and I'm comfortable to say Lycos is one of them. It's not like the opportunities will go away.'

Many analysts believe the opportunities may also flow the other way, with big media companies courting Lycos in the knowledge that both management and its largest shareholder are open to a deal at the right price.

Davis maintains that it is Lycos management who hold the trump cards, and that they will bide their time before committing to another mega-deal, no matter who initiates it. In the meantime, other matters – smaller acquisitions, alliances and partnerships – have continued to keep the Lycos name in the headlines.

Bob Davis continues to do what he does best – make deals.

And so it came to pass. In May 2000, Lycos was bought for $12 billion by Terra Networks of Spain. Despite this, it is Davis who becomes CEO, running a $500 million-a-year internet empire with 50 million unique users in 37 countries. It is a remarkable turnaround on the situation he found himself in just 12 months earlier.

Staying close to the consumers is the fun part of what I do

2

Jerry Yang
Yahoo!

Size matters

There's not a standard job description that comes along with founding a company like Yahoo so my job keeps changing. But what I've focussed on is really being part of the executive team with Jeff Mallett and Tim Koogle. The three of us really form the management team; they obviously have more operational roles and run the company while I tend to focus on strategy a little bit, and a bit on policy issues, especially dealing with future strategy.

I do a lot of PR and media relations. But what I really enjoy doing is staying very close to our business product team and seeing how can we improve travel, how can we improve finance? For me also, staying close to the consumers is the fun part of what I do.

I don't have anybody reporting to me which is something I think is really important because I play a role where I don't have any sort of proprietary interests. My only interest is trying to be of value at the center, organizing anything from product people to sales people to engineering people.

It's a unique role that I don't think could exist outside of Yahoo.

Introduction

When it comes to sizing up the competition, there is one name that provokes instant respect across the internet market – Yahoo.

Across a raft of measures, be it branding, hipness, earnings, marketing or strategy, the Santa Clara, California, group scores among all its peers, and remains the one to catch and watch.

Its 1999 results confirmed its star status. Net income quadrupled in the fourth quarter to $57.6 million, while revenues jumped from $91 million to $201 million. During December, daily traffic increased to an average of 465 million page views, compared with an average of 167 million page views per day in December 1998. It was a performance reflected in a stock price that reached an all-time high as it entered the new millennium.

Yet these are unsettling times for Yahoo. The takeover of Time Warner by AOL has put Yahoo firmly in the bid frame, prompting fresh inspection of an internet strategy that has eschewed content and delivery systems for an independence in services and platforms.

It is a strategy rooted in Yahoo's culture. The company was, and still is, the ultimate net start-up, founded in 1994 by two Stanford students – Jerry Yang and David Filo – working out of the back of a parking lot. With its anarchic name and message of can-do on the internet, the company has cut its own path to success. However, as the internet changes and new strategies are required, much of the management's willingness to adapt the business to these new environments will dictate Yahoo's continuing success.

The formation of Yahoo!

Jerry Yang, now 31, was ten when his family moved from Taiwan. His father had died, and his mother emigrated to the USA with her two children. He believes the importance of this move in terms of his development cannot be underestimated:

'It was probably the most significant event of my life, with being married being a close second. But especially from a perspective of being an entrepeneur, being able to experience the business culture in the US was a unique one.

'The US is special in that an immigrant can do what I did and be part of it. And not only me – but Jeff Mallett (Yahoo chief operating officer) is a Canadian. In fact, I would say that most key people at Yahoo have a relationship of being a first or second generation immigrant.

'It's clear that I am only an example of what could happen to people if they find the right place and the right opportunities and go for it.'

Yang believes the diversity and ethnic mix at Yahoo has played an important part in the company's development:

'I do think a lot of people who are new to the US tend to have a diversity of cultural background. In my case I was raised in a Chinese family and have a lot of values that are fairly Chinese and Eastern. Whereas my education, training and my business instincts are mostly Western. So I think that that type of diversity can be a good thing, and reflects on Yahoo as a global company that just happens to be congregated in Silicon Valley.

'I don't think necessarily it's an advantage or disadvantage because there are plenty of people who are born in the US that are very successful. But I think in our case the diversity really is a big part of our strength as a company.'

Yang had met David Filo at Stanford University, California, in 1990. He takes up the story:

'David was in the graduate school when I was still an undergraduate, being a teaching assistant at a couple of my classes. So I met him then but I didn't really get to know him until I joined the graduate school doing research in the same lab.

'We started hanging out together and spent six months in Japan. Being students and putting yourself in a poor environment really bonds you. In fact, a lot of people we met at this time ended up being in Yahoo too.

'Being in the same research team, which was relatively small, you get to know everybody very, very well; they were a second family and David was, and will continue to be, one of my best friends.'

Yang describes the discovery of Yahoo as an 'accident', while he and Filo were supposed to be working on a postgraduate thesis:

'It wasn't so much of a grand plan. In fact, it was quite accidental. We started with some listing of websites that he liked and some I liked, and I wrote some software.

'I said why don't we put it into a database and we can both add and change and delete from it. And that list grew from a few hundred to a few thousand. We thought: this is a website to get to other websites – maybe we should put it on the web?

'This was 1994 and before we knew it we had people from 90 countries logging in and then telling other people to try this thing out. It wasn't called Yahoo at the time – it was Terry's Guide To The World Wide Web. I'm glad we didn't keep that name.

'It was really a gradual thing. People thought it must have been some grand plan but it wasn't. It was built by people saying this is great, I love your search engine, but you have got the law section all wrong, here's how you do the law section. Or I'm a physicist in Geneva and here's how you fix your astral physics section. So we got help from all over the world and you get pushed by that kind of demand.'

Although Yahoo may have been an accident in Yang's eyes, he and Filo both had designs to do a start-up even while they were at college:

'David and I both got the entrepreneur bug. One of the reasons we were in the research group was that we thought by joining an outfit that had spawned a lot of entrepreneurial companies, we would benefit.

'We were involved in the design automation because at the time we joined there were a lot of start-ups in that area. We figured if we got a PhD in this subject we could go and start up something like that.'

>> we never thought Yahoo could be this big

However, as their interest in the internet grew, the two students were spending more and more time examining the business potential of the new medium. But not Yahoo. 'That was the funny thing. In the summer and fall of 1994, while we were maintaining Yahoo and growing it as a hobby we were writing business plans about other internet businesses because we never thought Yahoo could be this big.'

The Yahoo! business strategy

By 1995, Jerry Yang and David Filo had at last realized that the business with the most potential was the one they were fiddling with as a hobby. The business plan they wrote this time was to stand them in good stead – a strategy of building a brand around a piece of technology that everyone would want to use. Yang explains:

'We have been consistent with what we wanted to achieve right from the start; our strategy has never really changed. We didn't view ourselves only as a search engine, we saw ourselves as a brand before we knew what a brand was.

'Coming up with a name like Yahoo was something easy for people to remember us by. We didn't hire a branding consultant, we didn't spend thousands of millions of dollars trying to market this thing. People remembered it, people thought that we knew that the landscape of the web was going to change and trusted us.

'From 1995–6, it was obvious that websites were going to become more sophisticated, people were going to want more out of them. So we were able to change with our users. As users got more sophisticated we got more sophisticated, so we never just focussed on one aspect of what the portal functionality is.

'We also knew that in order to be successful we had to find the right strategy. The first part of this was that our brand was more important than the technology itself – we maintained the brand to be something very flexible. This enabled it to migrate from being a search engine to content provider to commerce player to communications provider – we do all these different kinds of businesses.

'The second part is that we found a strong management team. We were very fortunate to have found a group of people equally passionate about the internet but who had different skill sets. That really helped to grow the company, really worked as a team. It wasn't one guy directing the traffic, it was all of us reacting and trying to grow the business at the same time.

'Thirdly, we had a business model that worked as advertised if you excuse the pun. The point is that if we had a great brand, management team and product, but didn't have a great business model, we would not have been as successful. I think that the whole internet now is being viewed as much more than just sort of a medium or vehicle – it's also an economic phenomenon. And to have companies like ours go through the kind of growth that we are, but also achieving this profitability, is a key reason why people look at us and say, "Hey, these guys have really separated from their competitors".'

Why did he think that the Yahoo team got 'it', the *raison d'être* of the internet, and others didn't?

5 ways...

Jerry Yang
broke the
rules

1   Realizing that the internet needed a mechanism for organizing it and using the power and accessibility of the web to involve a wide variety of users to develop that.

2   Recognizing early on that building a brand on the internet would be a winning strategy.

3   Bringing in an experienced management team and being willing to delegate.

4   Recognizing the power of the 'free' business model on the internet, and developing the advertising-driven strategy.

5   Adding more and more free services to keep Yahoo at the forefront of the internet portals.

'I think we understood how big we could be. In retrospect everything we thought was going to happen happened, but five times greater. But I remember David making a very astute observation which we stuck to very early on, and that was that the internet needed an organizer. The internet is always going to be decentralized, it's not going to be one group or one company that's going to be in control.

'So our philosophy was that if the internet got big we were going to have to get big; if the internet didn't make it we weren't going to make it.

'We were focussed on helping people be organized. It meant you had millions of pieces of documents of information on the one hand and millions of people going on the web on the other, and how do you help them find each other. It sounds simple now, but at that time, you just don't know how much things will change. You have to remain really flexible in order to make that goal a reality.'

But it was one thing to come up with a smart business plan, quite another to then offer services for free. How did they come up with that as an idea?

'You have to remember that at this time, say '94, we offered this as a hobby to Stanford's university network, so it was still very academic, very research-driven. But then we got some venture capital and we had to come up with a business plan – we had to actually think about this as a business.

'The first question was how are you actually going to make money from this, and we had a choice: we could charge people for using us or charge somebody else. The conclusion was it was much more important for us to keep an audience who wanted to come back to us and keep it free as much as for heritage as for anything else. So we focussed on how we could derive some revenue from other means.

'The advertising model was just emerging, just being tested on the web and I think it was kind of a wild bet back then to say hey we're going to base our entire business on this advertising model. If you go back and read our prospectus or our history, I mean, read the 'Big Risks' section – like advertising industry's not for the internet, it may never work but we would rather take that chance than pissing off our users and getting them to feel like we'd sold out, like now we have to charge you etc. etc. So that's an important philosophy even to this day.

'We really don't have any services that charge people. You look at the amount of functionality we provide, as a whole, it's an amazing amount of things you can do for free. At least if you pay to get on the internet you can get it for free and we are really good at taking revenues from advertising and marketing.'

In addition to these sources of revenues, e-commerce is becoming an increasingly important part of Yahoo's strategy:

'We offer a lot of services to our users to make shopping easier for them, but we also offer a lot of services to merchants who want to sell the products on the web. In effect, we play an intermediary role, enabling users to find the things they want to buy on the web, while enabling sellers to find the users that want to buy from them. It's good for them and it's good for us – we don't handle the transactions directly, but we're an enabler. And we do that in a bunch of different ways in which people find shopping on the internet compelling.

>> e-commerce is becoming an increasingly
important part of Yahoo's strategy

'There's also a business model that gets us into servicing clients from a store front, kind of renting out store fronts, that sort of thing. But in the end it's a fairly simple consumer proposition, i.e. you can find anything you want to buy on the web, which is, I think, a very good extension from where we started.

'In the US, we have had a Yahoo shopping section that's been up and running for almost 18 months. We also have Yahoo auctions which is the second largest auction platform, and we have Yahoo travel which millions of dollars' worth of tickets are being sold on every month.

'For example, in September, the amount of transactions we enabled – meaning the gross products and services that were sold directly on our Yahoo shopping, auctions and travel platforms – was well over $100 million. That's just in one month, so it's very much happening as we speak. We expect that number to grow dramatically because the amount of consumer spending on the internet in the US is rising dramatically.'

The business-to-consumer revenue model operates in a variety of different ways. Yang explains:

'The business model over the next few years is mostly going to be a percentage of the transaction done. But we do offer different models. Some small stores don't want to do transactions for a percentage of sales, they just want to pay rent. Others say well if you give me a certain amount of volume I'll pay you a certain amount of fees. So it's a blend but I think conceptually the more traffic we drive the more successful our partners are and the more successful we will be.'

1   Maintaining its management team. As the internet moves into its next phase of development, the temptation for experienced managers to depart for new challenges will be strong.

2   Further, as Yahoo continues its rapid expansion, particularly internationally, increasing management resources will be a vital ingredient to success.

3   A tie-up with a media/telecoms company to boost Yahoo's distribution and content is inevitable in the wake of the AoL/Time Warner deal. Picking the right partner to fit the company's culture is essential.

4   Continue to focus on what it does best: free services, strong on finance, community and search.

5   Continue to innovate. This continual desire to reinvent and refresh itself is a key reason that Yahoo has kept ahead of its rivals.

5 hurdles...

for Jerry Yang and Yahoo!

There is also a business-to-business e-commerce strategy:

'One of the companies we acquired this year (1999) is called broadcast.com and this does two things. One is they have a lot of rich media, audio, video streaming, content, and sports games. So from a consumer standpoint, you can listen to a ball game, and watch a movie, etc. But the other side of their business, which is very innovative for us, is enabling us to get into business services. What they do is they help businesses conduct events. For example, if a company has a conference call, most are broadcast over broadcast.com. So, although it's small right now, we do have a growing business that is focussed on the business enterprise sector.

'Ultimately we're still going to be more informational rather than infrastructure-based, we're not going to go and deal with setting up computers and setting up networks and setting up heavy software. It's really more of an application arena we'll be part of, but it is a growing area.'

Yahoo!'s working culture

How joint founders split their roles is always a source of interest for outsiders – and a necessary issue to be sorted out by those involved. In Yahoo's case the two founders have no defined roles – both Yang and Filo are: 'Chief Yahoos' – although each tends towards a particular side of the managerial and technical divide.

>> The working culture of Yahoo has contributed
significantly to the company's success

'David and I have similar roles, but he's much more on the technical side,' says Yang:

'He is the one that really is behind the way that we are organized from a technology standpoint. If you look at Yahoo we served up 385 million pages a day in the month of September – somebody has got to be in the back figuring out how to get all these pages served up as fast as we can. David is the guy who believes in being the architect of how we distribute all this information in an efficient way.'

Meetings with his other managers are a constant occurrence, chiefly because they all sit close to each other in the famous Yahoo cubicles.

'Jeff Mallett and I sit next to each other, so we talk all the time. In Yahoo, everybody has cubes, so we hear each other on everything, we yell across the cube. Tim Koogle (Yahoo CEO) is next to Jeff, so it goes Tim, Jeff, me and our CFOs next to me so we hear each other all the time as well.

'We have what we call a hallway culture – everybody has cubes, and more things happen in the hallway than in formal meetings. And that's the way it's designed to be and that's the way it should be. When you have a meeting just to make a decision then you become bureaucratic and you slow down.

'We are getting larger and you have to keep fighting these sort of tendencies of becoming more bureaucratic by really pushing down the decision making to the organization, so you do not have to sit there and make every major decision or even small decisions.'

The working culture of Yahoo has contributed significantly to the company's success. The founders' laid-back and *laissez-faire* attitude, combined with a rigid focus on the company's strategy, pervades the business. Where does this come from?

'Again some people call it the internet culture, but when we started it wasn't. The informality is almost driven by the necessity of our business. That requires us to be responsive to our customers all the time, and everything else is built around that. That's how as an organization we got to be so horizontal. So if a customer complains then they don't have to go through four levels of people before you can give them back some answers. Because on the internet you lose that customer.'

The Yahoo! partnership strategy

Yang describes himself as 'very paranoid' about his competitors – but also sees this as another significant factor in what drives him:

'In the US, I would say that the media companies are very much in the picture at the moment. They have done a number of things to try to be in the internet space. We also have competitors in specific segments, such as eBay and auctions. We also compete with a lot of vertical players – I don't think people realize that – that are very good, so where do we stop?

'Ultimately we don't operate by fear, we operate by the need to be competitive in areas that we have decided to be in. What we need to do is execute because Yahoo today has a great franchise with our audience and they use us because they trust us and what we need to do is continue to be able to offer services that people trust. It's almost that simple.'

In the context of the AOL/Time Warner deal, Yang's views on partnerships, although made prior to the annoucement, are instructive. It is also a reminder of just how skillful the company has been in building its business with so little original material:

'I always talk about how we built Yahoo through partnerships because we don't produce any original content – we don't have writers and reporters and cameramen and things like that. What we end up trying to do is through a series of partnerships, whether it's on the content side, whether it's on the distribution side or business model side, you have hundreds if not thousands of partners.'

On the subject of dealing with just one media partner, Yang says: 'So far we haven't had any desire because I think we have been able to work with multiple partners so that our brand and our independence and our ability to offer our users choice have been the best value proposition. If we had only played with one player that would have taken away our value proposition.' He adds: 'We don't need to go exclusively with one group or another. I think that partnerships in our world today do not necessarily have to be exclusive in nature because the web by itself is something that is so open and free-flowing that it actually works against you.'

International expansion has been another success for the company – testament to the strength of the Yahoo brand:

'I think we are in 20 countries, and it's where I spend a lot of my time, especially in developing new markets. But we have always been very internationally-focussed.

'For example, we started Yahoo Japan when there were just 40 people in the whole company. What other group would think about starting a Japanese subsidiary when you're 40-people strong? We're now Number One there.

'We've also done very well in Europe. We have been there for three years and were one of the first internet companies to enter. Now it seems like every other day you get a new internet executive here, but for us that commitment happened early in helping build our business.'

It is a commitment that has continued. 'It's something we stress every day,' says Yang:

'We stress in the US that we have to be global and by global we mean that we have to adapt to each marketplace. That is the challenge.

'I think we have done a great job in making sure that we hire local people and I define how global a company is by how many employees are local. If you look, for example, at the concentration of Europeans that we hire, it's clear that we have devoted a lot of our resources, time and energy to not exporting US technology or people. It's about exporting ideas.'

It's like being an artist, it's just that innovators are painting on a different canvas "

3

Jay Walker
Priceline

Storming the barricades of commerce

I'm not driven by frustration. As an innovator, you are excited about contributing to making people do things in a new way. It's fun innovating when you can help people do things they could never do before. There's a real sense of value – I guess pretty much the same way a doctor must feel. It's like being an artist, it's just that innovators are painting on a different canvas.

What does drive me is that if I do innovate and do a great job, I can make a real difference and change a lot of people's lives for the better. Obviously it's not about the next dollar – that's not appropriate for me at this moment. But I have investors who say, I'm confident that you can deliver for me.

Introduction

Net revolutionary or slick salesman? Jay Walker is a subject who divides people.

To some, the 45-year-old New Yorker is simply a smooth-talking marketing man who has taken his pitch on to the internet and struck gold. To others, he is a visionary, reinventing the way commerce is conducted, as vital to society's development as Thomas Edison was in his day, and worth every cent of his $5 billion fortune.

Critics level two main charges against Walker and Priceline, his internet company. The first is that the heavily loss-making website, which invites visitors to name the price they want to pay for a variety of goods, from airline tickets to hotel rooms, is not financially viable. Even if it does turn profitable, critics argue that it will never be sufficient to justify the company's stratospheric market capitalization.

The second charge revolves around the issue of patents. Walker is nothing short of obsessive about protecting his assets – including intellectual ones such as business processes. His company, Walker Digital, has 25 patents approved and a further 225 pending. This includes a patent for the 'name-your-price' process underpinning Priceline's business.

This has brought Walker the kind of vitriol usually reserved for those heading for the penitentiary, rather than the internet Hall of Fame. How, the critics ask, can you patent a way of doing business? Bill Gates for one is not waiting to find out. Expedia, Microsoft's on-line travel business, has also launched a name-your-price service for airline tickets. The software giant says it is confident it can win any case brought by Walker Digital. Legal proceedings are now under way.

The formation of Priceline

Suing the world's biggest software group does not daunt Walker. Indeed, if confidence is a prerequisite of the entrepreneur, he has it in spadefuls.

The day we met, he had just left the stage at an e-commerce conference in London where he told a stunned audience of mostly British would-be entrepreneurs to tear up their business plans: the Priceline model held the future of web commerce. It was a riveting performance. Walker, gesticulating wildly with a rapid-fire delivery, combined the religious fervor of a Billy Graham with the vision of an Arthur C. Clarke. Fact or fiction, there is no doubting Walker's conviction and passion – and these facets pepper all his conversations.

It is hardly surprising to discover that the entrepreneurial spirit runs deep in the Walker psyche. His father was a self-made real estate developer, his college-educated mother held several sales positions.

The young Walker was encouraged to take risks and to do things differently. His family's middle class wealth enabled him to travel frequently and at the age of 16 he toured Europe on his own. The work ethic was also deeply imprinted. 'In my family getting bad grades was never an issue – the issue was that you were not trying hard enough,' he recalls. 'My father always emphasized learning over results. All those things had a real impact on me.'

After college, Walker was determined to start his own business: 'I was always looking for new ideas, different avenues to try.' By the time he had launched Walker Digital in 1992, he had founded around 20 companies. 'Some of them even succeeded,' he jokes. In fact, the most successful was a business that enabled people to renew magazine subscriptions via their credit card – a fairly revolutionary step in US financial services.

There were less successful stabs at art, conference and business services companies.

However, Walker had an early obsession with technology. While he refers to himself as a marketer and salesman, it is his love of technology that often permeates his recollections: 'I was an early adopter of computers. When I was at college I took a summer off to learn to program an IBM 360. I also owned one of the first Macs, and I've been a fan ever since. I remember Prodigy, the Videotext revolution, and so when the internet came along I was a very early user.'

So here was a crucial crossroads – the young entrepreneur of middling success with a fascination for technology suddenly discovers this new technology-based medium, the internet. But surprisingly, it was not the internet as such that caught his imagination, but the issue of patents.

Walker's constant search for a big money-making idea had led him to explore the use of cryptography in casinos. 'I realized that the cryptography industry intercepted the casino industry quite dramatically,' he exclaims. Pursuing this notion led him to examine the US patent system: 'I learned that the patent law was much broader than I or most people understood it to be. People knew you could patent life forms, but not things like business methods.' Walker takes on the look of an Indiana Jones discovering the Holy Grail: 'I thought, if you could patent business methods that were truly unique and novel, you could own them. That became the basis of Walker Digital.'

Inspired by his discovery, Walker Digital has registered patents covering a whole host of business operations, from postpaid travellers' cheques to on-line gaming to 'different business methods relating to forward options in the airline industry, and other industries.' He won't elaborate, believing that to do so will tip off rivals eager to second guess his next move. However, expect another Walker Digital initiative shortly – the company has hired a chief executive to explore commercialization opportunities for a range of patent applications.

5 ways...

Jay Walker
broke the
rules

1   Dared to patent his business processes.

2   As an outsider, he took on the notoriously protective airline industry – and
    won.

3   Went to the brink of bankruptcy in order to call the airlines' bluff.

4   Took the name-your-own-price model to other areas of business, again in the
    face of adversity.

5   Displayed an inordinate self-belief in the face of market cynicism and
    hundreds of millions of dollars in losses.

Patenting a business method, like Priceline's name-your-own-price, is straightforward common sense as far as Walker is concerned: 'You can patent anything that meets the tests of patentability – useful, novel and non-obvious. Those are the primary tests in layman's language to secure a US patent.'

The challenge, he says, is to make the business method non-obvious: 'It was not obvious to have a method of purchasing where you go on-line, name the price, agree the terms, put up your credit card details, and be bound to it if two or more sellers agree to your terms. Prior to Priceline, no one had ever done anything like this before.'

Walker was angered by Microsoft's 'blatant' move, particularly since he discloses that the two companies had been in discussions over closer co-operation. No other company has yet challenged Priceline's patent. He admits, however, that it would take a company with deep pockets to do so, and they do not come much deeper than Microsoft. Walker mutters darkly about the triple damages that a patent infringement can carry, but admits the vagaries of the US legal system will probably tie the case up for years. In the meantime, Microsoft can continue to build up its name-your-price business while Priceline can only look on. 'It's not my ideal choice, but the triple damages make a good second,' he says resignedly.

The debate about the use of patents to fight off competition has tended to overshadow events at Priceline. However, now almost two years on, the business's progress has something in it for supporters and critics alike.

The Priceline concept

When Priceline launched in April 1998, the concept appeared at once ludicrous and intriguing. The company invited visitors to its website to bid the price they wanted for airline tickets. The customers got cheap seats, the airlines flew full, Priceline took its commission and everyone was happy.

With US airlines flying with 500 000 empty seats every day, Walker thought it was a sure thing. He was wrong. His lack of reputation in the notoriously closed world of the airlines and a booming economy prompted a cool response from the industry:

>> When Priceline launched in April 1998, the concept appeared at once ludicrous and intriguing

'They just would not buy Priceline as a solution. But they get a lot of people coming to them saying, "Hey, you've got a problem and I can fix it for you." And the good ideas and the bad ideas don't sound so different.

'What they were essentially saying to us was that they did not believe that we were going to be a significant player, because in their experience very few people outside of the industry ever get to a prominent position.'

The airlines were also fearful that Priceline would become a rival internet destination to their own websites. They saw the internet as an ideal opportunity to sidestep the established distribution system of travel agencies. Then, explains Walker:

'Priceline comes along and tells the airlines, we're going to create a marketplace where we're going to decide which customers they get and at what price. To which they replied, we're not at all excited about that – we'd rather they just came directly to us.

'But we told them, if they come to you, you can't give them the price they want because that would destroy your price integrity. You need someone like us to serve as a shield for your pricing and therefore serve as a brand and a price.'

The message fell on deaf ears. But Walker is understandably forgiving in hindsight: 'They didn't behave unreasonably towards us. In fact, with the exception of one airline, all the others sent teams of people to see us.' Walker continues:

'I talked to virtually every senior executive in the airline industry and I found them to be remarkably concerned about the changes in their industry and the effect the internet was going to have.

'They were simply not thrilled that Priceline was going to deal with customers in a completely new way. I can't say I blame them.'

The result was agreements with just two smaller airlines – TWA and America West – and a business looking in a forlorn state, even before it had launched. Walker decided to start the service anyway. 'I took an enormous risk launching Priceline, both personally and as a company. It took a lot of guts,' he says with characteristic honesty and immodesty.

Walker's gamble was that even if Priceline could not fulfill many of its customers' ticket requirements, the demand would be so great that the airlines would come to their senses and sign up.

Some $15 million was earmarked for the marketing campaign and, in typical Walker style, the 'chief innovator' persuaded Captain Kirk from 'Star Trek' to lead it. In fact, the actor William Shatner refused at first to meet with Walker, who was forced to pay him an appearance fee so that they could meet in a Manhattan bar. One can only picture the scene: the portly but smooth Shatner boldly going on a journey into Walkerworld where no other man had gone before. Within half an hour, Shatner had waived his $500 000 campaign fee in favor of stock options. These are now said to be worth some $7.5 million.

Priceline launched in April 1998 with Shatner reading the Walker-written scripts in radio broadcasts inviting customers to name their own price for airline tickets. In reality, the system was not such a bargain for customers. The airlines – admittedly only the two that had initially signed up – would offer seats to Priceline at discount prices, usually on off-peak flights, and often involving a stop-off. Priceline would then match the seats with what customers were willing to pay: if the two did not match, or Priceline did not make money on the transaction, the customer went away empty-handed.

> >> In reality, the system was not such a bargain for customers

Nevertheless, Walker guessed right – the response was overwhelming, with more than one million Americans trying to buy tickets. However, in order to satisfy even a small proportion of these, Priceline was forced to break its own rules and buy tickets on the open market, often above the level being named by customers. Only around one in 14 customers succeeded in getting a ticket in the first six months of Priceline's operations, and the company was also forced to subsidize each ticket by an average of $30 each.

Paying people to fly? It was an enormous gamble in terms of both building up the business and brand and forcing the airlines to the negotiating table. Three months after launch and with the company hemorrhaging cash and still with only a handful of airline partners, the critics were licking their lips.

But Walker is nothing if not nimble. He desperately needed to bolster Priceline's credibility, and in August 1998, persuaded Richard Braddock, a former president of Citicorp, to take the job of chairman and CEO. Walker stepped aside to vice-chairman. Braddock was rewarded with a hefty 10 percent of Priceline's stock.

The Delta deal

This was almost immediately followed by the breakthrough the company so desperately needed – a deal with a major carrier, Delta. But the agreement with Delta owed more to the airline's shrewd view that Priceline needed it, rather than vice versa. As a result, Priceline was set onerous conditions as part of the deal. These included warrants over shares amounting to some 12 percent of Priceline's stock. However, Priceline got its critical mass, and other major carriers soon followed.

The company has used the same stock incentive for its other airline partners. At the end of 1999, United Airlines, US Airways and American Airlines signed a stock option deal with Priceline, joining Delta, Continental, Northwest, TWA and American West.

Walker denies that Delta was the company's saviour:

'What secured Priceline's success was that we had what every business needs and wants – customers. We had thousands and thousands of people a week saying, here's my credit card, I want to buy an airline ticket. We'll go any time of the day on any airline, I won't change it, I won't refund it, I just want to go.

'If it hadn't been Delta, it would have been someone else. It was inevitable. It could have been American or United. We were talking to all of them.

'We had customers, the airlines had excess capacity. We demonstrated we could satisfy demand that we could immediately turn into revenue.

'If you were an airline, how would you respond if I said I had $5 million of business a week for you that would go on any flight you wanted at any time of the day? You'd say, "Step right in Jay, let's have a chat!"'

Easy words in hindsight. But the terms of the Delta deal point to a company desperate in the summer of 1998 for a helping hand. Walker admits: 'Everyone has doubts, that's human nature. There were days when we'd get up and say, this has got to end, these guys have got to give!' He con-

5 hurdles...

for Jay
Walker and
Priceline

1 Legal challenges to the business patents. Success could open the way to increased competition – and puncture the company's share price.

2 Proving the business model can be a profitable success.

3 Sustaining the Priceline brand in the face of mounting losses.

4 Improving margins while expanding into new business areas.

5 Combatting an increasing trend within some industries to use the internet to match their supply and demand trends more efficiently.

tinues: 'There were just days when you know what you're doing is right, but nothing is happening. Having patience can be very expensive, but we had no choice. Like in a strike, our mutual interest was to come together, and it was only a matter of time before we did.'

Walker also had concerns over the economic climate: 'Airlines were flying record capacities with bumper profits recorded the year before and so they had less need than ever for a service to fill their empty seats. We could not have launched at a more difficult time.' He adds: 'Fortunately, our investors were sophisticated and really understood that we had solved the problem; they knew that in things of real scale and real innovation you need to have the courage of your convictions to hang in there. And hang in there we did.'

Tough though the summer of 1998 was, Walker believes the company achieved much in a short period:

'We launched in April and by October 1998, we had millions of dollars a week of demand. True, we were turning down a lot of that, much to our customers' frustration.

'But guess what? Customers knew there was no guarantee we were going to get them a ticket – they viewed it more as a gameshow than anything else. So they didn't win the game, but they were coming back.

'So if you launched in April and by November you'd gotten some of the largest companies in the world to agree to give prices to you below anything else, I think that's a pretty good speed.

'Now sure, it's not a good speed if you're losing $2–3 million a week doing it. One needs the courage of one's convictions in such circumstances and to feel comfortable that you're going to be able to prevail.'

With Delta on board, Northwest Airlines followed shortly afterwards, and the execution rate for customer tickets shot up. The Priceline model could begin to work in the company's favor, with the business actually taking a commission on tickets sold.

In addition, big name investors were drawn to the company following the Delta deal. George Soros, the billionaire investor, and Paul Allen, Microsoft co-founder, were among those who put in $55 million of private equity at the end of 1998. It was a smart investment. Three months later, the company went public in a spectacular IPO that saw the stock placed at $16 and close at $75, valuing the company at around $10 billion.

Latest initiatives

The fact that the share price has held up since the IPO is in part a reflection of Priceline expanding into other areas of business. Hotel rooms, mortgages, cars and groceries have fulfilled Walker's belief that a customer-driven, name-your-price business model can be adopted to a whole range of goods and services:

'Priceline was never about the airline industry. We are about excess supply and pricing. The patent does not speak to airlines at all. The patent speaks to commerce, to a whole pricing system. We are not an airline-specific solution – it was just the first thing we chose to price.

'We have said very loudly that by the end of 2000, through our licensee The Warehouse Club, we will seek to price all categories of retail. We hope to have 25 000 stores in our network in a wide variety of categories.

'We have made no secret of the fact that if we can price travel, mortgages and cars, we can probably price anything, and we will.'

Among the latest initiatives to be tackled are phone calls. Priceline plans to introduce name-your-price long distance and international calls.

It has struck a deal with Net2Phone, a US telecoms group which uses Internet Protocol (IP) services to transmit voice and data signals. Other agreements are likely to follow with other service providers. Priceline says the service will generate a lot of repeat business, as well as introducing more people to the name-your-service method of business which would have a knock-on effect in relation to its other offerings.

Another initiative is a name-your-price car rental service. AutoNation, which includes the Alamo brand, and Budget have both signed deals with Priceline to supply cars for the new venture.

These initiatives are certainly being reflected in the group's operating figures – although scepticism remains among some observers over the long-term viability of the business. For example, in its 1999 third quarter figures, losses jumped from $19.8 million to $102.2 million. Although the company said that some $88 million of this was related to warrants issued to Continental Airlines, it was a reminder to investors of the unwelcome surprises internet companies can spring.

At the same time, revenues jumped from $9.2 million to $143.6 million, a 16-fold rise, deflecting most of the flak from the unexpected high losses. During the quarter, the number of airline tickets sold rose from 38 000 the same period the year before to 624 000. This was also a 50 percent increase from the second quarter, 1999. Priceline also booked 180 000 hotel room nights, a 95 percent rise on the second quarter. Car sales doubled on the same basis, while mortgages increased by almost half.

Daniel Schulman, the Priceline president, told an end-of-year internet conference that the company would break even in 2001. He predicted that the company would earn $800 million of revenue in 2000 as more services were added and it won more repeat business.

One service to be announced at the end of 1999 was Perfect YardSale. Here, vendors offer second-hand goods for sale via the Priceline site. It is a regional service so that potential buyers can travel and inspect the goods before they buy them. This saves on shipping costs and means that Priceline does not have to act as a trusted third party.

While such a service is not unique – most of the auction sites have a version – Perfect YardSale is different, according to Walker, because there will be far more sellers than buyers thus enabling the latter to beat the vendors down on price.

Not surprisingly, Walker Digital has several patent applications pending on the new service. In addition, the new business is likely to be spun out of Priceline, being separately managed and attracting its own investors.

Perfect YardSale evolved through the ranks of Walker Digital, which, like Priceline, is based in Stanford, Connecticut. Walker explains that there are some 30 people who work for the group, which is run completely separately from Priceline. The Walker Digital staff are constantly conceiving and evaluating new business ideas and processes.

Once an idea has been accepted for evaluation, a team of perhaps four or five employees will set to work on it. Brainstorming sessions follow, with the idea being kicked around, challenged and questioned. In some cases, an outside expert is brought into the process to further the discussions. Finally, when the idea has been formulated into a formal business proposal, it must pass the ultimate test – the destruction process. This involves the rest of the staff, i.e. who are not involved in the project, meeting up to destroy the idea. If it passes that passage of fire, patents are applied for.

I put it to Walker that he was a deconstructor of business processes, a skill that enables him, and his team, to strip down markets and methods and to discover the revenue-generating drivers behind.

'I wouldn't call it deconstructing, although that is not an inappropriate word. What I am is a marketer. Most people who are in the internet market are technologists. They're enamoured of the technology, they look for solutions and they look for problems to which they feel they have solutions.

>> Priceline's success so far owes much to its ingenuity

'But as marketers, we ask what are the problems and how can we solve them. We like to think of ourselves as firmly focussed on the fundamentals of the marketplace as opposed to the superficiality of the latest technology.'

Priceline's success so far owes much to its ingenuity. In its widespread appeal to consumers to 'name-their-own-price', it is in fact solving a fundamental business problem for many industries. So, airlines get their seats filled, hotels their beds booked and telecoms companies, their empty lines used.

The challenge for the management remains – how to turn a high-volume low-margin business into profit. At the same time, competition is intensifying: more and more airline tickets are being sold on-line, the hotel industry is under increasing attack from web-based agencies, and telecoms costs are dropping across the world.

Walker Digital's patents may go some way to protecting Priceline, but, as Microsoft has shown, those companies with their own sense of conviction and deep pockets can undermine even that monopoly.

That said, Priceline's future remains as intriguing as ever. And Walker's next move is unlikely to be any less fascinating than those he has made to date.

It's got to be different, it's got to be creative, it's got to be executable

4

Jim Barksdale
Netscape

Proof that adult
supervision works

Introduction

Here is a dilemma few executives have to face. Your company has just been bought for the odd few billion dollars by industry giant AT&T. They want you to stay on and offer you several million dollars as a golden hello. Next, Bill Gates calls up. He wants you to be chief operating officer of Microsoft, one of the most powerful positions in the most influential company in the world. Finally, a headhunter gets in touch. He's got a start-up company in Silicon Valley, valued at $2 million, and wants you to be the CEO to a bunch of college kids with a bright idea.

For Jim Barksdale, the hardest option became the easiest choice. The year was 1995, and the 51-year-old had had a lifetime of big corporations and fat organizations. He had made enough from the AT&T acquisition of McCaw Cellular to retire.

And as for Bill Gates: 'I didn't want to be number five in a two-man organization,' Barksdale recalls. He didn't even turn up for the interview with the Microsoft chairman. Nor did he return the call when Gates approached him again. 'That would have ticked him off I should think,' says Barksdale, smiling at the memory that the two would shortly become bitter adversaries, culminating in the famous Department of Justice case against Microsoft in 1999.

Instead, Barksdale met with the venture capitalists behind the start-up, Netscape, and took the biggest gamble of his career. At an age when most successful businessmen would be contemplating improving their golf handicap, Barksdale moved from Seattle to Mountain View, California, as CEO of the new venture.

Joining Netscape

In returning to technology, Barksdale was completing the circle he began after graduation. He joined IBM as a data processing salesman, based in Memphis, from which he retains his southern drawl. He then began learning about the technology business from within the biggest computer company in the world.

Promotion followed and Barksdale moved to New Jersey. It was the first significant factor that was to kick-start his entrepreneurial career. 'Even though I'd been promoted, IBM was paying me less money than when I was a salesman because I was no longer on commission,' he recalls. 'And I remember thinking, if you're successful you have to move, and I had these little children and I didn't relish the thought that they would have to keep changing school.'

There were other contributing factors to his eventually quitting IBM. Some close friends had decided to start their own business and had invited him along. In doing so, they were following a famous but rare example. 'Ross Perot had left IBM and made a lot of money starting EDS in the late 60s – an article described him as the fastest richest Texan ever,' remembers Barsksdale. 'Prior to Ross, no one ever thought about leaving IBM and I think he made us aware that we had a value, this was a new industry, people were willing to pay for your services. So it was a combination of all those things coming together.'

If he hadn't been promoted would he have still quit IBM?

'That's debatable, but I think so. It was getting to be predictable. But it was a great place to work, IBM. Great people, great training, God it was terrific. But it just looked like a long life of one job after another. That was just me. It wasn't everybody.

'My father had worked for a bank half his life. That was the norm, that was what was expected. People worked for IBM in the same way. I became aware that I could do better.'

What Jim Barksdale looks for in an internet entrepreneur

Passion and a good idea and a good team. We get about 30 proposals a day for businesses to invest in. Some of them are brilliant and some of them you just wonder about. The kind of things that separate the good ones from the great ones include, for example – is the idea a really great one; is it different; you're not just following the guy in front of you; the world doesn't need another search engine; let's not bet on one more type of e-commerce that's already been done. So it's got to be different, it's got to be creative, it's got to be executable, it's got to go against a definable market that's wide enough and deep enough to produce a really big revenue opportunity.

So that's the business. On the other side, who's the team? There are some people you would bet on even if the idea's not great because they're the type of folk who'd keep working it, move it a bit to the right, then left or come around from behind, but they would not give up. They have a look about them that's half crazy. Only a fool would pursue an idea after everyone else has told them they couldn't do it.

The other thing we look for is for those ideas that fall into areas in which we feel we have some expertise. We are what we like to think of as a full service VC firm, in other words, we'll come in and we'll help you, help with finance, serve on your board, recruit – which is always a big thing for start-up companies – we'll find you a good head of marketing or production whatever. The thing we bring to it is we've been there and done it. Most VCs haven't. They haven't actually run a business. That's one of the reasons we get so many requests and proposals – they like to think, and I'd like to think, that we could bring something to them through experience that's beneficial to them. A number of things we have already done are beneficial and they sing our praises and tell us we're the best investor they've ever had.

The business he and his friends started consisted of buying and selling computers. He admits it was not particularly successful, but it taught him a lot.

Another venture followed, Cook Industries, a computer systems group. This was sold to Federal Express, a small but fast-growing parcel delivery group, and Barksdale went with the acquisition.

During his ten years at FedEx, he rose to be chief operating officer. These were formative years for Barksdale's growing ambitions to marry technology with enterprise: 'Federal Express taught me an enormous amount. Taking a relatively small organization to a huge corporation, training, managing, motivating large groups of people.'

Innovation was at the core of the Barksdale years at FedEx:

'We developed our own tracing and tracking system which was really the core competency of FedEx then and now. I would argue that we were among the first industrial companies to use computer systems to differentiate our products. We realized that the information about a package was as important as the package itself.

>> Innovation was at the core of the
                        Barksdale years at FedEx

'Our competitors at the time, who'd been in business a lot longer than us, they poo-pooed all this. So we had a headstart for a number of years before they came round to our way of thinking and put their own systems in. As a result, it was a marvellous learning experience, it was a lot of fun, we were the first in the world with a number of innovative developments.'

The reason he was so successful at FedEx, Barksdale says, is due to the innovative nature of the company, a culture developed by Fred Smith, the chairman. 'Probably the finest leader I have ever known,' is Barksdale's tribute to the man who he says remains a close friend, as well as continuing to be a boardroom colleague at the delivery company.

Barksdale's next move was to be the number two at McCaw Cellular, Craig McCaw's mobile phone business. Based in Seattle, the company attracted the attention of AT&T, the long-distance phone giant, which eventually bought it for $4 billion in 1994. 'I was given the job of CEO of AT&T Worldwide,' he says. 'But I didn't want to work for a big company like AT&T. Great company, great people. But I didn't plan on staying.'

There were several approaches after the takeover from some of the biggest names in the technology industry for senior positions in their organizations. This included the Microsoft offer mentioned earlier.

The Netscape approach came from David Byrne, a headhunter and now venture capitalist with Benchmark Capital. Barksdale recalls:

'At the time I remember reading this article in *Fortune* magazine on the top 25 hot new companies and one of them was this one down in Mountain View, California, called Mosaic.

'I mentioned to my wife that this was a real neat idea. I'd messed around with the internet myself and I was a home user of proprietary networks of one sort or another. I was struck by the idea of a universal browser that could really give access to mere mortals.'

A visit followed from Jim Clarke, who founded Netscape with Marc Andreesen, and John Dore of Kleiner Perkins, one of Silicon Valley's biggest hitting venture capitalists and Netscape's chief backer. They agreed to wait while Barksdale wrapped up the AT&T/McCaw deal and, three months later, he joined Netscape as CEO. He recalls: 'At the time, this start-up was worth around $2 million, but I got a very nice piece of equity which is what I wanted and a fascinating group of people to work with. It was a great idea – we weren't sure how we were going to make money from it, but it certainly seemed like one hell of a product.'

Rapid growth for Netscape

Barksdale hit the ground running. He knew that the success of the Netscape browser depended on getting it out to market as quickly and as extensively as possible. However, the threat from Microsoft soon became apparent:

5 ways...

Jim
Barksdale
broke the
rules

1 Turned down a multi-million dollar deal to stay at AT&T, and the opportunity to become chief operating officer of Microsoft, in order to join upstart Netscape.

2 Ignored proper budgetary controls in order to let the business expand quickly.

3 Gave the technologists at Netscape the freedom to innovate.

4 Gave away the company's main revenue earner for free in order to increase market share.

5 Sold out to AOL at the right time.

'The week I arrived, we released our first commercial product, distributing it over the internet. But it became obvious over the next six to nine months that Microsoft had very different plans for this. They caught on to what the potential of this new platform was, they knew they didn't want it to stay independent and in business.

'Gates said in an interview in '95, if we give away our browser, we still have the revenues from our other products. If Netscape gives away its browser, what else have they got to charge for? I later confronted Bill about that quote in front of a US senate hearing and he said he was misquoted.

'But the point was the business was just starting. By the time I got here we had 100 people, and had already released the first product, although we had no revenue. And then in the first quarter we had $2 or $3 million revenue, the next quarter $8 million, the next $20 million, the next $40 million – we were the fastest growing revenue engine the world had ever seen.

'A lot of people don't know that about Netscape – we were profitable by our third quarter. By the time we were at full run, we were doing $600 million a year. That was more than companies like Yahoo hit after several years in business.'

Barksdale's purpose at the company was to bring a level of direction and control:

'Well we joke about adult supervision, but I was able to get the team to work together, define what it was we were going to be and what we weren't going to be, what our market was, how deep it was, how wide it was, what was addressable, how do you go after it, how do you set your mission, how do you promote yourself, how do you hire great people, how do you budget and finance, how do you raise capital.'

While many of these were skills he had built up over his years in business, there was one thing that caught Barksdale completely by surprise – the incredible growth of the business. He recalls:

>> The rapid growth of Netscape meant that
conventional business rules no longer applied

'It was exploding around us. There's no amount of experience that can prepare you for that kind of thing.

'All I could do was to try to establish some rules as to how we were going to operate so we didn't get lost and ahead of our supply wagons.

'For example – one of the things that bothered me when I first got there – they loved to make a decision one week then come back a week later and go back over it. I said: "Stop this." The first rule is – if you see a snake kill it. Don't call committees.

'The second rule is – don't go back and play with dead snakes. Don't waste your time on things that you've already decided. Even if it's wrong, we're just going to keep on going.

'The third rule is that all opportunities start out looking like snakes. Some of the hardest things to do, if you can do them, are the greatest opportunities.'

The rapid growth of Netscape meant that conventional business rules no longer applied:

'We came up with a whole new way of budgeting a business that I'd experienced before – because it was obvious we had to do something.

'I said, if you have this many sales this quarter this'll be your expense budget next quarter, rather than coming up with year-long budgets and so forth which I had historically done.

'We did these short budgets because we were at risk of letting our own prejudices, backgrounds and pasts tell us how fast the business should grow.

'My fear was that our own lack of imagination would stifle the growth. So I said let's just let it grow as fast as it'll grow. We'll figure out how to pay for it later.

'So we did it on the basis that that month's sales budget was next month's expenditure budget because if you're growing you can do that and the difference between one quarter and the next becomes your margin. That worked, but I'd never seen that done before.

'We decided to let it rip. This was summer 1995, and we were starting to get a lot of interference from Microsoft who were determined not to let this thing succeed.

'Despite all that, we became very good and productive at exploiting opportunities – selling the first major internet and intranet software that businesses put in in the world, for example.

'We grew the business into an international one within six months of being here. We built a whole new division that built application software, grown in our first year to maybe 900 people, and the third year we were 2000 people.'

America Online (AOL) acquires Netscape

In November 1998, Netscape shocked the internet market by agreeing to be acquired by America Online. That the doyen of net counter-culture was succumbing to one of the medium's dominant players was seen by some observers as a sign of the growing commercialization of the internet.

It was true that Netscape's bruising battle with Microsoft had taken its toll. But Barksdale was aware that Netscape's other business – its Netcenter e-commerce portal – also needed wider and more substantial support if it were to realize its potential. So, by partnering with AOL, Netscape gained a substantial backer for its e-commerce venture, and receive a significant boost to its browser business.

For AOL, the move gave it one of the net's biggest technology brands, which also saw an important alliance cemented with Sun Microsystems. It may have been a sad day for supporters of diversity on the web, but for the parties involved, the executives were in no doubt of the importance of the move.

On reflection, did Barksdale feel that Netscape had achieved its potential by the time AOL acquired it?

'I think we'd exceeded our fondest hopes in many areas. We missed a few, but given the situation we were in I thought we'd done very well.

'By the time we closed in March of this year (1999), the company was worth $10 billion-plus, that's in a period of 48 months and there's probably not more than a handful of companies in the history of the world that have done that.'

AOL, he believes, brought Netscape the ability to market its product to the widest possible audience, as well as giving it more financial muscle:

'The one thing we needed was a bigger distribution arm, and the obvious opportunity there was AOL. So when they came calling, I thought that was a very fortuitous thing for us. I didn't regret that. I thought it was best for the employees, certainly best for shareholders and we had a bigger entity behind us to protect us from capital erosion.'

Barksdale left Netscape after the AOL deal, in March 1999, a very rich man. Indeed between July and October of 1999, he sold AOL shares he had received as part of the takeover worth a staggering $96 million.

What next for Jim Barksdale?

What the man with the Midas touch was going to do following the sale of Netscape was a matter of intense speculation. He could have had his choice of jobs among the raft of big computer companies anxious to embrace the internet. Or take retirement on his wealth of funds.

However, early in 1999 he established a venture capital outfit, Barksdale Group, and he divides his time between his home in Aspen, Colorado, and the Silicon Valley headquarters of the new venture. Two former Netscape executives, Quincy Smith and Peter Currie, are partners in the business which includes in its investment portfolio HomeGrocer.com, an on-line grocery store, Escalate, Listen.com, MyCFO.com, Respond.com and Tellme Networks.

The last is potentially the most exciting of these. Ironically, it marries the talents of two former foes: Hadi Partovi, who was involved in the development of the Microsoft Internet Explorer browser, and Mike McCue, vice-president of technology at Netscape. Tellme was founded by the two men early in 1999. They have developed software that enables telephones to access the internet through simple voice commands. These commands will enable users to access a wide range of web content, such as travel, news and weather information.

Barksdale has also been pursuing political interests. He is an adviser to George W. Bush, sitting on the presidential hopeful's Technology Advisory Council. This is a forum for developing policies for the technology industry, as well as for the wider economy. Michael Dell, CEO of Dell Computers, is chairman of the panel, while John Chambers, CEO of Cisco Systems and Ray Lane of Oracle are also members. Barksdale also co-chairs TechNet, a bipartisan lobbying group that seeks to influence legislation on technology.

I'm the Chief Meddler, I do all sorts of different things

5

Jeff Bezos
Amazon

Building the net's biggest brand

I'm the Chief Meddler. I do all sorts of different things. I try to spend the vast majority of my time on customer experience issues, so I'm heavily involved in design meetings for new versions of the websites. I help with product development – that's where I enjoy spending my time most and actually where I do spend the majority of my time. But I help with everything. Last holiday season, we were understaffed and everybody in the company ended up working in the distribution centers – not only that but they brought their spouses along as well. So there we all were working the graveyard shift! My wife and I were there, packing and shipping. That's the kind of company we are.

Introduction

It starts like a drain, a low rumbling, then a sudden explosion. The Bezos laugh is something to hear and behold. It happens suddenly and frequently. It's as if the founder and CEO of the web's biggest retailer still can't believe his luck, that people believe in him as some kind of messiah of the net, hanging on to his every word, pointing at him in awe, cherishing his every move.

It is an impossible dream come true. Bezos has become a cult figure on the web. He may not have the technological genius of an Andreesen, or the marketing guile of a Yang, but he had the vision to be first to market and the tenacity to stay there.

Amazon.com is the name with the biggest resonance in e-commerce. From nowhere, the Seattle-based company has shot to the top of the net, losing hundreds of millions of dollars and creating a phenomenon in the process. It is a startling story. One in which self-belief and almost divine inspiration has succeeded in turning established economics on its head. How still the sages of Wall Street shake their heads and predict the company's downfall – and yet still it maintains a valuation running into billions of dollars, exceeding those of its established, and profitable, bricks and mortar rivals.

Jeff Bezos is the other geek from Seattle. He wears chinos to work and has perfected a ruffled look that would not be out of place at a fraternity party. His face has a permanently surprised expression – until the drain kicks in, at which point he throws his head back in raucous laughter.

There is much in life that amuses Bezos, probably not least the $7 billion fortune he currently sits on.

The formation of Amazon

Bezos chose the name Amazon.com because it is 'the earth's biggest river and we would offer the earth's biggest selection.' What about the Nile, I ask?

'Well, the Nile is the longest river, but it is actually a creek in terms of volume compared to the Amazon. Did you know that 20 percent of the world's fresh water is found in the Amazon basin?'

>> Once the fixed costs of a website had been surpassed, profit margins would soar

Bezos, 36, came up with the Amazon concept while he was working as a strategist for a consultancy in Florida. The idea was a simple one: as the internet expanded, a retailer would be able to reach customers more easily and cheaply through the new medium. Bezos figured that for a bricks and mortar chain of stores to double its sales, it would take a colossal investment to build an equal number of new stores. However, for an on-line retailer, scalability was not going to be a problem in terms of capability or cost. Once the fixed costs of a website had been surpassed, profit margins would soar.

So Bezos quit his job and with his wife flew down to Fort Worth, Texas. Here, he picked up his father's 1988 Chevie Blazer and took off for Seattle, where they figured there would be a surfeit of web-hungry volunteers.

While MacKenzie, Mrs Bezos, drove, her husband bashed out the business plan on a laptop. There were no great ambitions when the company started. Bezos hoped that the on-line bookseller-cum-retailer would find a niche and become a thriving small business. 'I told all of our early investors, who were friends and family members, that they would lose their money for sure.' The drain starts, 'Anybody who could have predicted what would have happened would have been institutionalized!' He shakes with laughter.

Bezos famously targeted the book market as the first to experience Amazon's on-line challenge. His passion for excellent customer service meant that he refused to leave any element of the book-buying experience to others: Amazon would order, collect, and deliver all its customers' orders. This entailed building warehouses and employing a whole host of sales staff. In effect, Bezos's answer to the book industry was not so revolutionary, he was simply replacing one ordering system, the bookshop or mail order, with another, the internet. The rest of the system was the same. Except Bezos counted on the internet slashing costs, enabling Amazon to offer hefty discounts to its customers. Low prices were one element; a second to none service and great customer experience were the other.

It was the potential that Bezos unleashed through Amazon that enabled the company to quickly go public and saw the share price soar. Millions of people flocked to the site – and stayed. Amazon's diligence in creating a destination that stimulated book buyers is sometimes overlooked in the face of its discounting reputation. Indeed, it has increased sales and customers, despite the resolute challenge from other discount operators and high street names with their own web presence. It is an issue Bezos is keen to explain.

'I think there is one answer as to why we have been so successful and it is extremely simple in theory, but very hard to do in practice, and that is we are obsessed more than any other company with the customer experience. Every aspect of it.

'So when you first hear about Amazon from a friend, what you are hearing is part of the customer experience. All the way to when you receive the package, how easy it is to open, how easy was the website to use – things like one-click shopping, store-wide sales rankings, gift clicking, easy browsing...'

5 ways...

Jeff Bezos
broke the
rules

1 The first to recognize the power of the net in revolutionizing the retail sector.

2 Put customer service at the center of his strategy, recognizing that it would be the only way to get people to use Amazon, despite the lower prices.

3 Has built the biggest e-commerce brand through a strategy of hefty expenditure. Profits were always subordinate to the brand. Brave, even foolhardy, but even cynics admit it has been a phenomenal success in setting out to do what he said he would do.

4 Could have sat on his laurels. After all, the US book business has just turned profitable. Instead Bezos has taken the Amazon strategy into other areas of commerce, confounding critics in his wake.

5 Oversaw the development of proprietary software that would enable Amazon to stay ahead of its competitors.

Bezos lists a whole host of other plusses of the Amazon experience: 'All these things we incorporated to make it easy – no matter what you do – to find the thing you're looking for, and then to be able easily and quickly to purchase it. That sort of miniscule focus on customer experience is the reason why we have been so successful.' He continues: 'There are four things that internet customers care about – selection, ease of use, price and service, and you have to be excellent in all four of those areas. You can't pick one to leave out, and if you do you will not be successful.'

This, he believes, is doubly important in an internet business: 'Focussing on customer experience is the most important thing in any business, but it's especially important on the internet because word of mouth is more powerful on-line.' He sees this as a positive force, encouraging better service from internet businesses, because poor performances can quickly lead to demise, such is the power of the medium.

Latest initiatives

Amazon has expanded from books to compact discs to auctions, and now through z-Shops, thousands of different products, offered by different merchants. Bezos says this is the tip of the iceberg for where Amazon wants to be: 'Our long-term vision is to build a place where people come to find and discover anything with a capital A. We are not going to be able to do that alone – we are going to do that in partnership with thousands, tens of thousands, maybe even millions of third parties.'

This, however, could pose problems for Amazon. Firstly, utilising the services of thousands of partners could adversely affect the much-cherished customers' experiences. Equally, by trying to be all things to all people, the Amazon message of service and quality could be undermined. Bezos disagrees:

photo © Financial Times newspaper group

'We only want to be one thing and that is earth's most customer-centric company. This is our number one mission, and this encompasses three things. First and foremost, listen to customers and figure out what they want and how to give it to them. Second, invent and innovate for your customers – because it's not their job to do that, it's yours. Third, personalization: put each individual customer at the center of their own universe.'

Bezos's vision of a horizontal shopping portal is at odds with analysts' belief that the internet will develop into a more vertical model. Thus, for example, on-line financial service companies will serve that part of the market better than a broad-ranging portal such as Yahoo – or an e-tailer such as Amazon.

Indeed a recent report from Forrester, the US research group, forecasts that 57 percent of all on-line ad spending will move to sites focussed on one segment of the market – so-called vertical portals – and affiliate networks by 2004. This would be more than double the current figures.

Bezos remains unshakeable in his belief that he can maintain Amazon's reputation for excellence across any area of commerce: 'If you want to go to the best music site, you come to ours because it is the best. If it wasn't, you wouldn't come.' The reason for this is simple, he explains:

'We have a big advantage in trying to build the biggest music site because a lot of what is required is the same kind of infrastructure that was needed to build the best book site.

'It's things like one-click shopping, and gift clicking, and browsing features, and search functionality and ease of navigation and a whole bunch of things. Plus all the customer service facilities and customer service obsessions cut across both categories.

'So there are huge advantages for us. Obviously there are differences in every area of commerce. So in music, for example, the editorial content will be different to books – so that means you go out and hire the very best people in the music space.'

Bezos uses the analogy of Condé Nast, the publishing house, which publishes both travel magazines and women's fashion periodicals. 'They are a diverse company offering different titles,' he says, adding that Amazon's approach is no different. It is simply a matter of analyzing the market, hiring the right people, then creating the right environment.

A recent example of this is the group's deal with drugstore.com, the leading on-line drugstore. At the beginning of 2000 the two companies inked a multi-million dollar agreement to integrate a number of the companies' shopping features and create a drugstore.com shopping 'tab' at Amazon.com. Under the agreement, Amazon will receive $105 million over three years.

1 Extend and ensure Amazon's reputation for customer service to other areas of retailing.

2 Resource the scope of Amazon's operations in line with management ambitions.

3 Maintain Amazon's reputation as the strongest e-commerce brand in the face of intensifying competition.

4 Take Amazon forward to the next phase of the internet's development – namely television and mobile commerce.

5 Keep laughing in the face of mounting losses. Such optimism seems to do wonders for the Amazon share price.

5 hurdles...

for Jeff Bezos and Amazon

For its part, Amazon will make an additional $30 million investment in drugstore.com, bringing its total stake in the company to 28 percent.

Drugstore.com will also become the first of Amazon's partners to feature prominently on the group's website as a permanent part of its regular navigational structure. Bezos says that additional features that will make shopping at drugstore.com still easier – integrating Amazon's '1-Click' shopping, a shared shopping basket, and more integrated search and browse capabilities are planned for later.

The aim is to enable Amazon's 17 million customers to shop seamlessly between drugstore.com and other Amazon stores – with equally high levels of customer service. Bezos explains: 'We're working to make Amazon.com the only place where you can find anything and everything you might want to buy on-line – what you're seeing today is a completely new component of that strategy.' Bezos said at the time of the deal earlier this year in 2000: 'We chose drugstore.com to be our first partner with this level of tight integration because they obsess over customers the way we do, and we expect more arrangements like this when it makes sense for customers.'

Indeed, within days of the drugstore deal Amazon announced that it had agreed to acquire a 5 percent stake in Greenlight.com, which it said was the only on-line car buying company that gave consumers the convenience and control of on-line purchasing coupled with the support of a leading network of premier auto dealers. The Seattle group will promote Greenlight to its users – receiving $82.5 million over five years and warrants to increase its stake to as much as 30 percent.

Greenlight's proposition – offering consumers the ultimate car-buying experience – 'a no-hassle, no-pressure way to research, choose and buy exactly the car they want; 24-hour, 7 day-a-week customer service; and strong, ongoing support from local dealers during and after purchase,' fits in well with the Bezos/Amazon philosophy.

Luxury goods have also appeared on the Amazon site, courtesy of Ashford.com, a retailer of luxury and premium products. As with its other partnerships, Amazon made a minority investment in Ashford, together with a multi-million dollar marketing initiative and a strategic alliance. Ashford will sell a number of luxury product categories, including diamonds, watches, sunglasses, and writing instruments, through the Amazon sites.

Luxury items and collectibles have figured prominently in Amazon's expansion. Late in 1999, the company bought Back to Basics Toys, an online retailer specializing in hard-to-find classic toys. It was a typical Amazon purchase. The Viginian company had spent ten years cultivating a distinctive selection of classic, high-quality toys, as well as a loyal customer base. The acquisition added yet more depth to Amazon's Toys & Video Games Store, which has been rated top among on-line toy stores in a number of surveys. Bezos is proud to point out that the channel has been rated the best on-line toy store by MSNBC and Forrester Research's Power Rankings, and named a PC Magazine Editor's Choice.

Then there is the 18 percent stake in home furnishing e-tailer Living.com, Bezos's latest in a flurry of marketing and investment deals. This time,

Living.com will pay Amazon $145 million over the next five years for a permanent 'tab,' or store location, on Amazon's website.

Another millennium deal swiftly tied up was with Audible.com, which will pay $30 million over three years for promotion on Amazon. The latter will buy a 5 percent stake in the multimedia company for about $20 million.

Finally, one of the group's most prestigious tie-ups to date has been with Sotheby's, the famed art auction house. At the end of 1999, the two groups launched sothebys.amazon.com. The site has made available a broad range of art, valuable objects, and collectibles from more than 100 collecting categories. Auction enthusiasts can search for particular items or browse by category to find, discover, and buy special items of interest.

Plans for future expansion

Bezos's confidence in bringing in new partners is based in part in the enormous self-belief he has in the Amazon strategy, but also is a result of the success garnered in similar moves so far. For example, in November 1999, Amazon launched channels selling home improvement, software, video games and gift ideas. Three months later, the company announced soaring sales from the electronics and software business, and a total of six electronics products were included in Amazon.com's top ten revenue-generating items for all retail stores for the month.

Industry research backs up the Bezos philosophy on customer service. In December 1999, Amazon.com was ranked the No. 1 On-line Electronics Store by Gomez Advisors Inc., a leading provider of on-line research and analysis. In addition, Amazon.com tied for the top overall customer satisfaction rating among on-line electronics retailers in a December 1999 poll conducted by Harris Interactive, a leading internet-based market research and polling firm.

Bezos is laughing again. This time at my doubts that he can maintain Amazon's reputation if he insists on outsourcing much of the company's future expansion. 'We can't make Christmas ornaments as well as your aunty in Wales,' he giggles.

He returns to serious mode: 'What we won't do is ask our customers to put up with an inferior experience. In everything we do we start with the customer and work backwards. We won't even enter areas where we don't think that we can improve the customer experience.'

Acquisitions remain a possible avenue to new pastures:

'If we can find a great company that has the people in place that are focussed on customer experience as we are, then we will move for them. Those decisions are made pragmatically, however, there is no theory or formula. We look at the situation, try to understand whether it makes sense for us and then make a decision.'

>> Some analysts would like to see Amazon become
   the world's biggest e-tailer within its niche areas

Some analysts would like to see Amazon become the world's biggest e-tailer within its niche areas: books, CDs and the like. Auctions, collectibles, and cars make them understandably nervous, although Amazon's stock price has remained robust. There was news for both optimists and pessimists in the company's most recent results. The good news, and something that will give a huge fillip to Bezos supporters, is that the book business turned profitable for the first time.

However, losses ballooned. The company was in the red to the tune of $185 million in the fourth quarter of 1999, compared with losses of $22 million for the same quarter a year ago. Sales, though, trebled to $676 million. And new customers kept on clicking on, up by 3.8 million to 16.9 million during the quarter, with repeat customer orders representing more than 73 percent of revenues. Worryingly, Amazon's profit margins shrank to 13 percent from 21.1 percent during the same period in 1998 and from 19.8 percent during the third quarter of last year.

Amazon blamed inventory problems – but Bezos was unbowed in the face of any criticism: 'We're always going to err on the side of the customer. That's part of our business model.' The company also admitted that some of its newer businesses operated at a negative margin for the fourth quarter, meaning that Amazon sold items in these areas for less than cost. Nevertheless, Bezos says there will be no let-up in Amazon's expansion, despite the high cost: 'We continue to believe we are in a landrush period in this industry. We feel we are the most efficient e-commerce incubator in the world.'

When you're dead, you're going to be dead for a long time, life is too short

6

Christos Cotsakos
E*Trade

Courage under fire

I'm the head honcho and chief visionary. So I'm responsible for the future and making sure the spirituality of the company remains intact. But I stay involved on a day-to-day basis on everything – because you have to fly at 50 000 feet and you have to get your hands dirty in the foxhole. That's the way the internet entrepreneur works today. You have to be both. You have to know what's going on both on a micro level as well as a macro level because the two fit together very, very tightly.

I'm one of those weird guys – I can only sleep four hours, if I sleep more than that I can't function – so I'm up 18 hours a day and the net becomes great, because I can work with people all around the world, I don't have to bother them on the telephone. I love that intensity. When you're dead, you're going to be dead a long time, life is too short, I want to suck as much energy out of this planet as I can before my time comes. A legacy from Vietnam? Absolutely, I ran from Vietnam for a long time. I spent so much time destroying things that I eventually wanted to make up for it and build things. That is what we are doing now, so everybody can play against the preferred institutions, so everyone can play against the haves and the have not's. This is a way for me to pay back the community who were so gracious to me as I was growing up.

Introduction

Christos Cotsakos likes to joke that when he first came across VCs (venture capitalists) in Silicon Valley, his heart missed a beat. The last time he'd encountered the acronym was as a soldier in Vietnam 30 years earlier.

In fact, jokes and Vietnam are two distinct but essential facets of the E*Trade CEO. A vibrant and vivacious personality, Cotsakos, 50, is unlike any other internet entrepreneur by virtue of his background. A working class son of a Greek immigrant, he was a high school dropout, before finding glory and his will to live on the battlefields of the small south-east Asian country.

Like his contemporary and mentor Jim Barksdale, the former Netscape CEO, Cotsakos cut his corporate teeth at FedEx. He was recruited from the delivery company to E*Trade by the founder of the company, Bill Porter, in 1996. Since then, his tenure at the helm of the on-line broking group has been marked by rapid growth, but also growing losses as competition from traditional stockbrokers intensifies.

Morgan Stanley Dean Witter, one of Wall Street's biggest and most aggressive brokers, has been the latest to announce an on-line trading service to its clients. It joins Merrill Lynch, American Express, and other full-service financial firms muscling in on internet broking. The likes of E*Trade, TD Waterhouse, and Ameritrade Holding have responded by cutting fees by as much as two-thirds and doubling spending to acquire new accounts – spilling more red ink in the process.

Indeed, the figures are mind-boggling. Analysts estimate that the internet brokers will spend $1.2 billion this year on marketing alone – as much as the entire US cosmetics industry spent in 1998. E*Trade alone will spend $350 million on advertising in the next 12 months, including a $1 million first prize to the person who predicts the level of the Dow Jones Industrial Average by the end of 2000.

E*Trade's latest results reflect both the buoyancy and the competitiveness of the market. The first quarter fiscal 2000 figures saw daily trades rise 65 percent and 330000 accounts added over the same period a year previously. Revenues rose to $246 million but losses more than trebled to $38.1 million after spending on sales and marketing reached a hefty $119 million, double its previous level. This last figure equated to an average cost of about $289 per new account, compared to the $198 per new customer the previous quarter.

>> Bravery in the business world does not
        come much harder than on the internet

Losing millions of dollars and facing competition from some of the biggest names in world banking is a daunting situation. But from Cotsakos, a man who stared death in the face in Vietnam and who buried some of his best friends there, beams an optimism so bright that fear of failure does not appear to enter his mind. Bravery in the business world does not come much harder than on the internet. Losing other people's money carries with it a special responsibility, more so in a market where no one knows what the outlook will be in six months' time, let alone a few years. Whatever it takes, Cotsakos appears to have it in spadefuls.

Christos Cotsakos – a personal history

His first memory of making money was in the New Jersey neighborhood where he grew up. 'My brother loves to tell this story,' says Cotsakos leaning into me as if we're co-conspirators.

'I was in elementary school and we were very poor growing up and I was always looking at new and different ways to try and make money to help the family.

'Back in the '60s when you went and bought comic books, on the back you could order Christmas cards. In those days it was pretty trusting – they actually sent you the cards before you sent them the money. Could you imagine trying to do that today? I don't think so!

'And so I looked at it and thought what a great way to work: if I order a box of 12 at a buck and a quarter a piece and sell them, I get to keep a quarter, 25 cents. But that's really not a lot of money.

'So what I did was I ordered 100 boxes of 12 and I got all the neighborhood together and said here's what we're going to do. I'm going to give you 10 cents for every box you sell. I'm going to give me 10 cents for every box you sell because I'm going to orchestrate it, and we take 5 cents and allocate it to your mothers and fathers. So everybody wins.

'And we organized the whole neighborhood and we ended up selling about 150 cartons of holiday cards. Everybody made money and everybody had fun. It was the talk of the neighborhood and it was my first experience of how to organize and get things moving and how to manage at both the micro level, because I was selling, and the macro level, because I was organizing. And my first experience of how you piece the whole deal together. That was my first start – I was about 10 or 11 years old.'

The young Cotsakos had been raised in a business environment of sorts – his father ran a New Jersey diner. 'He was the best short order cook on the planet,' boasts Cotsakos.

He also remembers of his father: 'He never graduated from grammar school and was one of the most well read people you could ever want to meet. He knew everything about virtually every topic. Especially politics and especially history. He had to converse so he had to know. He was terrific.'

5 ways...

Christos
Cotsakos
broke the
rules

1   Recognized early on the impact technology could have on a big organization, in his case, FedEx. It was this foresight that took him to E*Trade.

2   Recognized the need for partnerships and alliances. Many start-ups want to do it alone. Cotsakos recognized, again early on at his time at E*Trade, that the company's success would be dependent on other companies.

3   The impact of the net on financial services was recognized by many in the industry, but few had the guts to build a brand, virtually from scratch, in the face of the biggest names in the banking world.

4   Understanding that the financial services market had suffered appalling customer service and making that the core of the E*Trade experience.

5   Tricking his way into FedEx by working for nothing.

Despite his early experiences and the inspiration of his father, Cotsakos was a poor student. He says he lacked direction, motivation and ambition:

'I basically flunked out of high school. I had a high energy level and a low tolerance level and got bored very easily. And I felt that school was just tiring and not very exhilarating and I think I cut the most classes of any student in my four years in the state of New Jersey. I think I also had more detentions, when I got caught, than anybody in the state of New Jersey.

'But I was one of those kids they passed every year just so I wouldn't be an annoyance if I stayed in the same year. They sent me to summer school every year and I actually flunked that as well. In my fourth and last year, my English professor was going to flunk me, which meant I wouldn't get my high school diploma.

'But then he found that I was working nights loading trucks at a grocery store. So he said to me one night when I was working – because he used to come from time to time – "It's of absolutely no value to flunk you and keep you in the school system because you'll never ever go anywhere. I'm going to pass you and give you a D which is one grade above failing and you can go back and do all these menial jobs that you're so well suited for." I said: "Thank you very much," and went on my merry way.'

Although angry at this treatment, Cotsakos admits he did not have much idea of what he wanted to do:

'I spent a year and a half doing a bunch of menial jobs. He was correct, I didn't know where I was going to go or what I was going to do.

'The only thing I did want to do was to fly jets. I loved technology and I loved aviation. So, I went to the air force recruiter and said, listen I'm Christos Cotsakos and I want to fly jets. He said, do you have a college degree, and I said, no. He said, do you have a high school degree, I said, barely. He said, do you have any references, I said, no. He said, well we just can't use you, but maybe the navy might.

'I thought I was pretty smart. So I went to the navy and said, I want to be a carrier pilot. A dangerous job. They asked me the same questions. Do you have a college degree, no. Do you have a high school degree, barely. Do you have any references, no. Why don't you go and see the marines.

'I did that, but they were out to lunch. The army guy was in the corner, you know one of those come on down types. The army always recruited. I said look I don't really want to join the army but I want to be a helicopter pilot. I was kind of moving down the food chain in aviation.

'He said we'll hook you up with an airborne division and you can be a parachutist. Then you can go to school because your grades aren't that good, the same college drill, you don't have any references, etc. And then we'll guarantee that we'll send you to be a chopper pilot. I said, great. He said, do you want to go to Vietnam. I said yeah, I want to find out what war is all about and see how that fits in.'

The year was 1967, and the war in Vietnam was beginning to grow in its ferocity:

'They said it would take nine or ten months to process my application, then there would be the training, so don't worry about it. Then they called like 30 days later and said, you know what son, you're in the army now. So then I had to tell my parents and they went crazy, and I had to tell my family and they went crazy because everyone was trying to avoid the draft and I was joining up.

'But I thought my life was going nowhere. I needed some discipline. Plus, I didn't want to miss the military experience because my grandfather was an OSS in World War II and I always used to sit and talk to him. He used to tell me about World War II and what happened. The *ésprit de corps*, the camaraderie, the teamwork and trust and those stories – a lot of things that are important to me.'

His experiences in Vietnam would change his life forever:

'In Nam, I found everything I thought about it had been wrong. I was a squad leader, a sergeant with the second 501st airborne infantry.

'I went over in December 1967, and it was terrifying. It was a bunch of young kids, in control of awesome firepower, scared 24 hours a day. It was about winning to survive another 24 hours. It was never about America, democracy, or preserving a way of life. It was surviving and winning with your team on that given day.

'I learnt a lot about who you trust, what's important to you. I used to think who you lived with was important, but I came away with who you choose to die with is very important. It's not about the good times, it is who is going to be with you in the bad times. So I learned about people, courage, mental and physical, teamwork –if you are going to be skilled at something you have to know that someone else's life could depend on it. I learned a lot about leadership – I ran a squad of 15 people.'

Cotsakos describes his life in Vietnam as 'a typical grunt'. His squad was in action frequently: 'We were seeing fighting almost every day. A lot of close hand-to-hand stuff, search and destroy, that sort of thing. Our unit was always engaged in big firefights. I was either walking point or circling behind enemy lines, the first line of defense, the last line of offence.' He shakes his head at the thought: 'It was an experience to be face-to-face with the enemy who was no older than me.'

He killed people?

'Unfortunately yes, I still have a lot of dreams about that, although it took 15 years to get over the worst. I could not talk about it. I had a pact with three friends who were all killed. It took years before I could visit their graves. I finally went back to Vietnam and got the dirt where one of my friends was killed, gave it to his mum, threw the coin over the bridge….' His voice trails away.

'Another friend who was severely wounded I heard from yesterday. Thirty years later and he named his first son after me, we talked and cried. We will get together in a couple of weeks.

>> Cotsakos was decorated for his bravery in Vietnam

'Out of the whole team of 100 less than 25 came back. It was devastating, they either became disabled or got killed. I got wounded. I spent four months in hospital – you learn a lot about physical pain, choice and what is important.'

Cotsakos was decorated for his bravery in Vietnam:

'I got a Bronze Star for valor for single handedly attacking a machine gun nest that had the whole company pinned down.

'Then I got an army commendation medal for valor. We were being over-run, and in a mine-infested area. The enemy had come near our camp and turned their big guns on us – it was chaos. Then they broke through our perimeter and were firing on us from behind.

'So me and my squad doubled back and attacked the enemy in our camp and managed to push them outside the perimeter. A lot of people got killed and I got a Purple Heart for the wounds that I received. There were so many heroes there that never got any recognition because nobody saw what they did. That's the unfortunate part about bravery, if no one sees you, you don't get the recognition you deserve. Everybody was a hero. Me, I was lucky, I came home.'

Joining E*Trade

A lukewarm reception awaited most returning Vietnam veterans, and Cotsakos was no exception:

'I tried to look for jobs, but most people were insulting at the interviews – being a war veteran had no value.

'A lot of people did not want anything to do with you. The last guy I saw was a bank vice-president, who said maybe he would consider giving me a teller's job. I never heard from him again.'

It was then that he got a timely break:

'My brother John, who is seven years older than me, helped the mayor in his election campaign. The mayor always gives out favors if he wins, so when he won, my brother said: "I am going to get you in to college." I said: "It's impossible, my grades are so bad."

'But he got me an interview at a state school and after one hour of the interview, I got accepted. I was at school the next day. It was incredible.

'I loved reading, I was more mature. I had decided what I wanted to do and what I wanted to be. I spent three years graduating with honors. And then I met my wife – we've been married for 27 years – it was unbelievable, everything changed in an hour time frame with something that was a favor for my brother for what he did. Otherwise who knows where I would have been today?'

Cotsakos's roller-coaster life was not over yet, however. His first foray into the corporate world after returning to college was also an interesting experience:

'I was going for my masters at UCLA in theatre and needed a job to get me through. I looked in the newspapers and there was this opening at FedEx. They were looking for cargo handlers, managers and sales people.

'I had just moved to LA and knew nothing about the area. I went down to the Marriott Hotel where the interviews were taking place with my

5 hurdles...

for Christos
Cotsakos and
E*Trade

1   Continuing to innovate in order to differentiate the company from its growing band of competitors.

2   Linking up with other service companies in order to widen E*Trade's ability to recruit customers and lower its cost of acquisitions.

3   Rein in marketing expenditure.

4   Roll out the E*Trade model overseas more aggressively.

5   Convert more customers into higher value users.

hair down to my shoulders, ratty jeans and three hours late. Well, everybody had gone except this group of people in the lobby talking about how their interviews had gone.

'So I went to the concierge and gave him five bucks, and said: 'Look, this Federal Express company. I know these guys.' I gave him a line of bullshit and got the FedEx guy's room number. I went and knocked on the door, a woman answered, I looked like a derelict.

'He came to the door, we talked for 30 minutes through the crack in the door, me trying to get him to give me a job at $3 an hour. I was working at Universal Studios at the time for $1.40 an hour, so I would have doubled my money. He opened the chain, gave me an application and said: "We give very few of these out, you're being considered." And he never called.

'I called them every day, but they had filled the jobs. So I got in my MG, and hung around at the airport, talked to the guys, started loading the trucks for nothing, finally they offered me a job after I had been there a week, as a casual cargo handler at $3 an hour.

'The rest is history. I worked hard, I loved the company, it was my growing up period learning about business with Fred Smith who rose to be one of the big division managers.'

Fred Smith was one of Cotsakos's great heroes:

'Fred was the first and last of the great benevolent presidents of companies. He had such a way with people for motivation, nothing would deter him from what he believed to be the right course of action.

'I learned so much. Fred was an ex-Marine, he was in Vietnam in 1967 when I was there. I had every job you could possibly imagine, from cargo handling to sales rep, customer services, technical service director, regional director, division head, vice-president, general manager, I worked overseas and in the US. I was blessed, I got to grow up in a variety of different environments and had the opportunity to learn a lot of different jobs from the best people in the industry.'

It was during his time at FedEx, one of the most technically progressive organizations in the US, that Cotsakos discovered a love of technology:

'I was a closet geek, although I'd never had a lot of money to get involved with it.

'I remember being at AC Neilson learning about consumer behavior, and it was there that we got involved in a lot of technology, mostly mainframe-based. We went to a desktop system and the internet was just starting, so it was an easy way to gain access without the cost and without the burden of the hardware. So I became enamored by it by accident based on the technology of the time.'

Cotsakos rose through the ranks at FedEx and developed strong views on how technology could improve operations. It was around this time, 1996, that Bill Porter made contact. The two men met and what was due to be a brief chat turned into a marathon session as they explored their views on how technology in general, and the internet in particular, would revolutionize many industries, not least financial services.

At the time, Cotsakos had been struck by the decision of Jim Barksdale to turn his back on the big corporations to take on the job of a start-up in Silicon Valley:

'I thought I was going to run the big battalions at FedEx. But it had also enthralled me that Jim Barksdale had gone to this company called Netscape. He'd gone from FedEx, to McCaw Cellular then to this little company. Jim was also one of my heroes, as well as Fred.

'So, Bill and I talked some more. I had done a lot of reading about the net, and I told him how I saw its usage – we ended up spending about 16 hours together, looking at things that I would change about E*Trade's infrastructure.

'Bill called me up the following morning asking me to come down and talk to some of the board members. I spent the whole day again; he called me up on Wednesday and said why don't you just run the company. I said yes.'

Difficult early days

Cotsakos explains how the company was beset by initial problems:

'Like all great entrepreneurs, he had a built an infrastructure that was very small and Bill had a lot of insights and they complemented mine. I had a huge vision of what I wanted to do – unfortunately, we did not have the money, the right people, or the right technology.' Worse was to follow:

'Bill thought he had lined up credit facilities to continue funding the company – until we found out there was no money! The company was in violation of the net capital rule. So we had to find $10 million in two weeks, or we were in big trouble.

'It was just an oversight, people promise you stuff that never happens. But nobody would give us the $10 million. Finally, I am down to about six days and we are in deep, deep trouble. I'm selling but nobody's buying.'

Among the investors Cotsakos sought out was Softbank, the Japanese group that specialized in internet investments:

'I say to my team members, "Look, just follow my lead, look smart, look confident, look like we know what we are doing."

'We sit down with the guy from Softbank. I said I don't have any time to waste. I need $10 million, I need it in six days, if you are not the guy who can make this decision thank you very much but I cannot spend time on a 45-minute breakfast. He said I can make a $10 million offer within six days if I like what I hear. We talked, we had a handshake deal, I had a $10 million investment in six days, I was able to go out on the road and start selling and the rest is history.'

That investment from Softbank staved off a crisis, but was not the solution to E*Trade's problems:

'We did not have the right infrastructure, and we could not recruit anybody, because nobody knew what the net was then, nobody wanted to come and work for $60 000 a year.

'Meanwhile, I had been making $2.5 million a year and my wife was saying how are we going to move from New York, now all of a sudden there is no money to move you, to Silicon Valley where the real estate is extremely expensive, and when we have a daughter in high school. My personal life was in chaos.'

So what, I wonder, was driving him at this time?

'I wanted my whole life to get back to a small entrepreneurial group like the camaraderie we had in Vietnam, where we could all have a common goal and vision. Eliminate all the bureaucracy and focus on doing something grand and do it right.

'Bill gave me shot to do that, he took a risk because I was not from the industry. I knew nothing about the security business. We had a good talk about what I thought technology could bring to the consumer. And where I thought personal finance would fit in a grander scheme. We almost had double vision, his and mine.

'There was an inherent drive in me to do something on a grand scale. To do something with a group of people who are very talented and driven. I love intensity. There was the spirituality, for all the crap I had seen in corporate businesses you could build your own culture.

'You could actually say this is what I would like to create as an environment, people would be proud to put their footprint in the sand, individually and collectively.'

>> E*Trade's latest initiative takes
investors' interaction to a new level

It is this constant desire to be stimulated that also attracted Cotsakos to take the plunge with a company in the internet space. To always be at the forefront of technology, to be nimble and to be prepared to change were part of his own business culture.

'What the net does today is it renders every business model, both those in cyberspace and those in physical space, irrelevant almost every 180 days. You have to continually reinvent yourself and the company, and rejuvenate what you are trying to do, so the intellectual stimulation in your capacity to be creative in a variety of different areas is enormous. This is a thrill.'

Plans for the future

E*Trade's latest initiative takes investors' interaction to a new level. Cotsakos explains:

'As technology becomes less complex and easier for people to understand, as narrow band becomes more broad band, as information can be delivered on any device at any time and all over the world, we can now provide people with non-stop customized and personalized financial information that will enable them to make better decisions and be better informed about their financial future.

'It's interactive. The whole system is designed so that if you want to use landline, or satellite, cable, or PC, TV, wireless, you can get that data whenever you want. It's all about info and news that allows you to make a decision and hopefully profit from it in the marketplace by making a smart transaction.

'It is also a way to build a huge financial command center that has every-thing at its fingertips from mortgages, insurance, stocks, bonds, IPOs, CDs, right down the list.'

An interactive portfolio will be the first initiative in 2000. Cotsakos explains: 'You will be able to access information, about your cheques, credit, allocate your funds, real time video streaming, managing your money, with instant chat and communication.'

Is E*Trade the only company to be doing this?

'Yes, to the extent we are. It is a huge data warehouse. The net is about you and me, about how well I can blend complex technology with com-plex human behavior and make you smarter, give you more choice, give you the ability to level the playing field. Whether it's shopping for a PC, a stock, getting a bank account, buying a house, it's all about the power of the individual and making you the center of the universe.'

Attention also needs to be paid to the delicate balance of partnering and making sure that your chosen partners are the right ones for your organi-zation:

'It's all about leveraging partnerships. One thing to beware in this environment is those who compliment you today compete with you tomorrow.

'Back to the military, there were no clear lines of demarcation, everything was blurred, there were no clear battle lines. The net is the same way. If you don't understand guerrilla warfare, if you believe in fixed objects, you think that is going to be a defense against the new empowerment of the new on-line consumer, you're sadly mistaken.'

Drawing on his Vietnam analogy, I ask who is Charlie, the US troops' nickname for the Vietcong enemy. Cotsakos laughs:

'I think Charlie is anybody who tries to intermediate between you and what you want to do. What they end up doing is taking a slice out for a big price of your time and life.

'People are saying today, "I'm mad as hell. I'm not taking anymore. If you want to charge me a fair price, I will look at your advice, but don't charge me 20–30 times what you should, because the cost of information is being accommodated." So people who misuse people's time or overcharge – that's who Charlie is.'

Whether E*Trade is the company that can carry this message remains to be seen. Cotsakos has done a fine job in building the company and the brand. However, the speed at which the bricks and mortar banks are waking up to the net is worrying – as are the huge amounts of money E*Trade is spending to keep ahead of the intensifying competition.

It is interesting to note the emphasis that Cotsakos puts on partnerships. Could an alliance with a large financial institution with little or no net presence be the way forward for E*Trade? It would make little sense for the high street names perhaps, but a less well-known institutional firm may see value in tieing itself to one of the strongest brands in internet financial services.

For E*Trade, such a move would enable it to reduce costs through the cross-fertilization of customers and gain access to the deeper pockets of a profitable organization.

I'm a Renaissance kind of person, I love to do lots of different things

7

David Hayden
Critical Path

Innovation as
a way of life

Introduction

David Hayden came to prominence in 1998 in *Burn Rate*, an entertaining if bitchy book by the journalist Michael Wolff of his attempts to take his internet company public. Wolff's bankers think it a good idea if he first merges with Hayden's company, Magellan, which he owns with the twin daughters of the late disgraced British media baron, Robert Maxwell. Wolff casts Hayden, husband to one of the Maxwell sisters, as a slightly feckless soul, forever at the mercy of the scurrilous family he has married into. That Hayden has survived not only such a character assassination, but also rebuilt his career around the next generation internet technology, is testimony to his powers of survival.

In fact, on meeting him, one is left in no doubt at all that here is a man it would be impossible to keep down. With his mop of mad scientist hair, and a mind that seems to compute a hundred different ideas a minute, Hayden is a restless bundle of energy. He gesticulates wildly, smiles readily and speaks with the conviction and passion of a self-made man thrice over.

We meet in the converted Victorian offices in San Francisco that are home to his latest venture, Critical Path, an e-mail management company. But not before he has kept me waiting for half an hour: a Stanford computer student has dropped in to run something by him – Hayden operates an open door policy for any budding undergraduate with a bright idea.

Ideas for Hayden are the currency of the future, and one senses he would be equally at home in a philosophy class or in the business environment. But here he has a clear advantage – the millions of dollars he has made

1 His enormous self-belief drove him on to set up Critical Path despite the indifference of the venture capital community.

2 Brought in key management at an early stage.

3 A belief that ideas are greater than the prevailing technology and that the latter will eventually catch up with his own demands.

4 Recognizing that the utilization of his talents lies in business development, not operational management, and bringing in talented people to compensate.

5 Using the notion of transporting a sick dolphin to come up with the idea of starting a benevolent VC fund. It was an enormous leap of faith and one that only someone with Hayden's will power could pull off.

from Critical Path, and other ventures, give him the luxury of turning ideas into reality. For the internet entrepreneur, it is a dream vocation.

The formation of Critical Path

Hayden grew up with a passion for architecture, and his first job was in property and construction. It was as a real estate developer and construction manager that he paid his way through college, ending up with a degree in political science from Stanford University.

Any entrepreneurial inkling as a youngster he attributes to his grandfather and uncle, rather than his parents. 'Neither of them were business-minded,' he recalls. 'My father was a lawyer and my mother was a social worker.' He continues:

'However, my grandfather and uncle were very entrepreneurial. My uncle always worked for himself and I can say the same thing. I've always worked only for myself my entire life.

'My grandfather was just a great, wonderful guy who was an accountant for the first part of his life and then at the age of 40 had a career change.

He bought a lumber company in Stockton, California, which grew into a very substantial business between World War I and World War II.'

Hayden's successful stint as a property developer might have continued, had it not been for his meeting Isabel Maxwell, daughter of the disgraced media tycoon Robert. The two fell in love and got married in the late 1980s. It was also to have benefits for his business career – and the reason he made the move out of property and ultimately into the technology market.

'Isabel's sister Christine was running a company called Research on Demand, and it needed some attention. She was much more of a creative publisher and she wanted some help sorting the financial side of the business out. So I stepped in and helped her turn things around, and we made it profitable in the process.

'I was doing this on the side while I was still running my property company. In the process I gained a lot of knowledge about on-line information and resources and how that might be delivered. In particular, I began to think about how you would gather information and deliver it to specific people in an on-line environment.

'That was partly my introduction to technology. The other part probably came from my own business experience, where I had created a whole set of programs that were easily usable by our field superintendents to track their jobs on a day-to-day basis.'

Not that Hayden sees himself as a technologist. The suggestion sparks an energetic response. His arms wave, he stands up, he sits down:

'I'm a Renaissance kind of person, I love to do lots of different things. I like to have my hands on a number of different projects at any one time. I'm a multi-disciplinarian. The first part of my life was taken up by doing things that were tangible, creating buildings. I did everything I wanted to do there. I didn't know a lot about technology, but that never stopped me wanting to learn.'

Confidence is not something Hayden has in short supply:

'I will dive in completely unafraid to take on anything. That's leading into some interesting things right now. I can present well, speak well, I'm reasonably charismatic, I can get people engaged in doing something. It's always been a trait. I've always been an over-achiever – I was a leader at school, and an eagle scout. I like to be first. I'm very competitive.'

His work with Christine, and his involvement with Isabel, led to the three exploring new business initiatives. Christine's company, Research on Demand, was involved in supplying research material to corporate clients and the issue of getting that information to time-poor executives was an intriguing one. It was an area that the twin sisters knew well. Business information and the supply thereof was something of a passion for their father, who spent millions of pounds investing in both content and delivery systems during the 1970s and 1980s as he expanded his media empire.

Hayden recalls:

'We began wondering about starting a new business. The three of us wanted to do something that was hopefully unique, and we latched on to the idea of the internet as a means to do that.

'We saw a huge opportunity to develop a directory of destinations on the net – there were fewer than 50 000 websites in 1992 when we started. Our first directory, one of the earliest guides to the internet, covered 1 000 websites.'

The venture was called McKinley after the highest mountain in North America. 'It was a cute metaphor for what we wanted to do,' says Hayden. Out of McKinley came the Magellan search engine, one of the first on the web. 'It was a pioneering effort of its time,' says Hayden proudly. 'Yahoo was not taking that approach until much later.'

However, being first to market in the burgeoning internet market of the early 1990s was not in itself a guarantee of success. With both subscription and advertising-based business models still being developed, revenues were tiny, while being in the forefront of this early technological revolution demanded large investment. Many early net pioneers were consequently forced to consolidate, to both cut costs and gain the sort of critical mass that would make them more visible.

>> Many early net pioneers were forced to
consolidate, to both cut costs and gain critical mass

By 1995, Magellan for one found itself in just that situation. Its advisers brought it to the negotiating table with Wolff New Media, a net-savvy content company from New York and headed by its eponymous founder. A tie-up between a search engine group and a web media business seemed an attractive combination. However, what started out as a merger of equals descended into a messy squabble between lawyers, bankers and investors over how much each party was worth. Magellan's 'burn rate' – the amount of cash it was using up above its income – was far greater than Wolff's, a fact used to great effect by Wolff's advisers who attempted to exact control of the merged group.

Michael Wolff, a former journalist, portrays himself as a pawn in all this, dictated to by greedy bankers and cynical investors. Hayden is cast as a desperate man caught between a high cost base and a receding revenue line. Behind him, like master puppeteers, are the Maxwell sisters, who are depicted as opportunists out to make a quick buck from a company fast running out of time.

It is all good knockabout stuff – although having had long discussions with both Hayden and Isabel Maxwell, their perspective is somewhat different. Indeed, for someone shown to be an arch-opportunist ready to take the money and run, Maxwell's subsequent track record argues differently. She has remained in Silicon Valley and, ironically, now runs an e-mail management company up against the business of her (now) former husband. Commtouch has grown into a $500 million business, while Maxwell herself has become a prominent figure on the West Coast IT scene.

The Wolff/Magellan deal eventually collapsed, as did Hayden and Maxwell's relationship. The search engine was sold to Excite in 1996 for a knockdown price. It is the only time in the meeting that Hayden comes anywhere near reticence: 'It could have been great. But I had no regrets about leaving – it was good for me to get out of the relationship with the Maxwell family.' He pauses and repeats, 'I have no regrets.'

Is that why it didn't realize its potential, because of the personalities involved?

'I think so,' he says. 'There was too much conflict internally.'

Hayden was left to lick his wounds:

'I took a couple of months off to think about what I wanted to do next. I had no idea what I was going to do, or who with. I had to do something, but I had some time to think about what that would be.

'I hit upon the idea in December 1996. It centred around the question, how would you create the equivalent of a certified delivery service for the internet? How would that happen? The idea possessed me all through December and January.

'I started the company (Critical Path) that month. I had no one working for me. I began to write the business plan, but not about a certified delivery service. The dilemma on my mind was this: on the internet the messaging takes place without any intermediary. You can send an e-mail and it will connect to a router that sends it out on the internet.

'It's roughly 97 percent successful, without any mediation from any human hands. Let's say the problem is that I want to send a certified letter or financial transaction to you. I need to know it gets there for legal purposes. But if I'm on AOL and you're on ft.com, I can't do it because you're on a different server system.

'There has to be a way that all of the transactions in the world can be certified, archived and stored. And there also needs to be an economy of scale of how mail is handled, e.g. I never thought it made any sense that

1 Hayden's wide spectrum of interests can give the impression that Critical Path is not the center of his universe.

2 Yet the company faces enormous challenges, not least reassuring both customers and investors that the recent breakdowns in the e-mail management service are behind them.

3 Technology is creating greater and greater server and software capacity. Outsourcing e-mail management must establish itself with the business community as a must-have service – and quickly before companies opt to do it themselves.

4 At the same time, competition in Critical Path's market is intensifying. Again, it must reinforce its reputation for reliability in order to remain at the forefront of the market.

5 Technology remains the key to the company's prosperity. Investment in its service is vital for profitability to become a reality.

5 hurdles...
for David Hayden and Critical Path

every business in the world was going to run its own e-mail server in some department – it makes no sense on an economic level.

'I wanted to provide a way of certifying delivery for a message and provide a better economy model of handling messages on the internet, combined with the knowledge that all communication is going digital, i.e. an internet-based rather than analogue-switched voice communication system.

'Knowing that the software part of the messaging is very complex, I thought there would be an opportunity to create a company that would be part of an industry that would be trusted in handling messages, certifying delivery and handling everything related to your identity on the internet.'

Hayden continues, almost breathlessly:

'It possessed me. I thought this is it; it would not let me go. Even with Magellan, well you can imagine the internet in 1992, wouldn't it be so helpful from an educational tool point of view, to create a directory so people could find out all different things? That was very exciting, but when I thought of this, this was even more exciting to me.'

Initial challenges

For Critical Path to succeed, Hayden figured that it would need to combine the technology of a new media company with the service element offered by traditional businesses:

'You need to have the trust and reliability of both areas of business, so that we are in the first place a service company. We need to be able to take all of our physical pieces that need to be sent digitally, and know they will get there. A service company has to guarantee that that is going to happen. It has to operate with 100 percent reliability.'

The challenge for the new company was twofold: create the technology to cope with such an awesome task as hosting millions if not billions of e-mails; and sell the concept to businesses. Persuading them that a third party will host and handle all their sensitive e-mail documents was going to be tough:

'Our message was that being a virtual host was the new model. That this would not hurt your brand. AOL is a brand, FT is a brand, and any user of those brands does not lose their association with that brand by going on our service because we invisibly mirror their domain address with a domain address on our servers. The reason we call ourselves the brand behind the brand is that we actually create a domain space to match your domain space, so we are the virtual host of your domain.

'But I knew that the idea of me giving my e-mail to this unknown entity was shocking. I knew, right from the start, it would be a large hurdle to overcome. But I also knew it had to happen.

'This is what kept me going: I knew at the end of the day, if you really look at how things are going to end up, it was a logical outcome – the economics spoke for themselves.'

Hayden's enormous self-belief and confidence at this time are all the more surprising given the breakdown of his marriage and disappointing end to his last venture. However, he says that his belief in the internet as a technological medium, and his own conviction of his ideas, carried him through: 'I just said I'm going to create the market and make it happen. And sell the idea that you are going to save money and get a better service. You don't lose anything by doing it, there is no security loss, you don't lose your identity by outsourcing to us.'

Even so, few people shared Hayden's vision: 'We were the first ones to think this through, but still couldn't get it funded. We had one VC who came to see us, I remember, in July or August of 1997. He looked at what we had and said: "Nobody will out-source their e-mail to you." I looked at him and said: "Fine, see you at the IPO." '

Fine words, but as Hayden himself says in his immodest fashion, 'Being a visionary doesn't pay the bills.' He continues: 'But I am someone who will execute on that vision – it's a combination of being determined to create that vision and working through it.' He repeats: 'If you don't do the work, it doesn't pay the bills.' Finally, he muses: 'The reason I went into building rather than architecture was that I wanted to create hands-on the vision I was designing. I am very much a doer, I guess.'

E*Trade signs up

Critical Path's breakthrough came with the signing up of E*Trade, the on-line broking company, headed by Christos Cotsakos. That was in April 1998 and it gave the company the credibility it craved:

'When we signed them up, it gave us a reference to sell into the ISPs (internet service providers). Christos saw the concept of outsourcing, the concept of the technology and the scalability of it, the ability to run the service in real time. It took another visionary to say we are going to go with you and we want to invest in you. That happened around the same time that the venture community began to understand the idea. But it was a gruelling process.'

But it was also a moment of achievement and pride:

'It was a great thing for me personally. Even though I was the chairman of Magellan, I think everyone looked at it and associated me with the Maxwell family. I didn't think it was fair, so I was proving to myself and the world that I could do it. That is what drives an entrepreneur, they all have a chip on their shoulder – that's one of the motivators.'

David Hayden, Christos Cotsakos, a dolphin and a billion dollar VC fund

How do you FedEx a dolphin? That was the challenge that Hayden and E*Trade's Cotsakos found themselves facing in 1999.

The result was a philanthropic technology fund for start-ups, which has already raised $300 million and could rise to $1 billion by the time it launches later in 2000.

The idea for the venture started after a marine biologist approached Hayden to fund the $75 000 that Federal Express had calculated it would cost to fly a sick dolphin from San Francisco to Florida for treatment. Hayden called on his friend Cotsakos to share the cost.

In the end, a phone call from Hayden to Fred Smith, the FedEx chairman, saw the bill waived. However, the incident stirred the two entrepreneurs into realizing the strength of their business links, and the need for some sort of trust fund that causes – such as sick dolphins – could call on. 'We are two successful, wealthy and smart businessmen who want to use our experience and contacts to make a difference,' says Cotsakos. The new venture, as yet unnamed, will replace the role of the venture capitalist in bankrolling new technology companies.

Hayden says the group will offer more generous terms than those usually given by early-stage investors and take a more active interest in the companies' success. Thus it will also act as an incubator to member companies, giving management and technical support. In addition, the operational and strategic management of the companies will be undertaken on different levels. Thus the start-ups will operate with two levels of control, one strategic and one handling the day-to-day affairs of the company.

Hayden and Cotsakos will utilize their extensive contacts to bring in outside experienced entrepreneurs to sit on the management boards. 'Nothing has ever been done like this before,' says Cotsakos. A network of around 150 companies is envisaged. They will be linked through these strategic boards, as well as through a technical infrastructure. In return, companies will pay a proportion of their profits to the trust fund for good causes. The proportion has not yet been decided, but may vary from company to company depending on their pace of development. As with most Silicon Valley start-ups, the aim would be to nurture them and take them to the public markets.

Cotsakos, a decorated Vietnam War veteran, hit the headlines recently when it emerged that he had earned $9.6 million that year, more than double his previous year's remuneration. The amount covered salary, bonus and stock options. E*Trade lost $54.4 million in the same period.

Hayden, an internet veteran of several years, owns stock and options worth more than $150 million in Critical Path.

Hayden today

Hayden's energy and enthusiasm are infectious. He puts it down to his enormous self-belief and his ability to inspire:

'I love where I am in my life right now. But I've always been a very happy person. I stay healthy, all those things you have to do. I'm just happy about everything.

'There're so many cool things going on I'm just fascinated. Here's another example. I got to meet the President of the United States in July at a small dinner. There were just ten of us. I was invited as a representative of the technology industry. The President wanted to sit down and talk about how to make a better website for the Democratic Party.

'It was at Senator Carey's house in Georgetown and the President and I sat right next to each other And he asked me to kick off the dinner.

'We'd been briefed by the heads of the Democratic Party earlier. They said: "We want this to be a great Democratic site and we've got all this great Democratic propaganda that we want to put out on a site."

>> Hayden's energy and enthusiasm are infectious

'And I said, 'Well, that's really a stupid idea. Why would you go through the trouble of building a website if you didn't want it to be from an entrepreneur's point of view. If I'm going to put a website up I want it to be the killer website. I want everyone to come to it. I want it to be the Yahoo or the Amazon of politics. You're not going to create that if you're just pitching to the Democrats. You should be pitching to the Republicans. You should make this "my politics.com".

'And they go, "I don't know. You should probably talk about that with the President." So the Senator asked me to kick off the dinner and I said, "Here's what we should be talking about." And we had a fantastic dinner. He's so excited about it!'

I suggest that Clinton was probably stimulated by the fact that there was someone in his circle who was not agreeing with him all the time: 'That's right. In fact a number of people called me after that who were at the dinner and said he's still raving about it. It's the first time since he's been President that he wasn't just talking and everyone was going "Yes, Mr President".'

The next time the President was in San Francisco was the day prior to my meeting with Hayden. He says his rapport with Clinton is such that he wasn't surprised to get a call from the White House for a meeting while the President was in town: 'He asked me and five other people to sit down with him yesterday to talk about the website and some other technology stuff. It was just fun.'

Hayden has handed over the operational side of Critical Path to his senior managers. It has left him free to do what he does best – energetically exploring ideas, listening to young graduates, developing new ventures, and, of course, talking technology with the leader of the Western world.

"The quality of the searching was always going to be the important differentiator for consumers"

8

Steve Kirsch
Infoseek

Altruism born of
technology talent

Introduction

Amid the jostling to be annointed as one of Silicon Valley's success stories, the tale of Infoseek makes for more sobering reading.

The search engine portal was founded by Steve Kirsch in 1993. Renowned for its smart technology and having the advantage of getting into the fledgling internet market early, commentators took it for granted – as the

>> The writing was already on the wall for Infoseek

group's successful IPO demonstrated – that Infoseek would fly alongside the likes of Yahoo and Excite. Yet, as early as November 1996, the group was announcing a revamp of its site and services, with the very same commentators asking 'What is Infoseek's strategy?'

There were early indicators of the group's shortcomings. In the race to develop on-line services, for example, that would eventually lead to the portal strategy, Infoseek was too often late to the deal. And while its rivals raced to ink deals with distribution and content partners, those struck by Infoseek failed to inspire the market.

This was very much the case with the deal that would ultimately spell the end of Infoseek. Its stock price languishing and in search of direction, the group linked up with Disney's ailing Go.com in 1997. The entertainment giant took a minority stake, but the writing was already on the wall for Infoseek. Within two years, the search engine was completely subsumed in the Disney empire and the Infoseek brand usurped by Go. Early in 2000, Disney signalled a retreat from the bruising battle to become an all-embracing portal against the likes of Yahoo and AOL, focussing instead on its entertainment strengths.

So where did it go wrong for Infoseek? Perhaps more correctly, in a market which was exploding and awash with capital, why didn't it go right?

In hindsight, its biggest problem was in recruiting and retaining management of sufficient calibre. In Kirsch, the company had a talented technologist, but lacked a manager of sufficient experience and a marketer of particular flair. Imagine a Netscape with an Andreesen but no Barksdale, for example, or an Excite with a Spencer but no Bell. Instead, Infoseek seemed to operate a revolving door for senior executives. Robin Johnson, the first CEO, resigned after 18 months, and was followed by a series of other senior management defections, including the CFO and the COO.

When we meet, Kirsch is in the process of packing his bags at the Sunnyvale, California, former headquarters of Infoseek. Go.com logos adorn every wall. The receptionist wears a Go label in her hair, while two women dressed as ballerinas distribute Go memorabilia around the building. It's a surreal movement, almost Stalinist in its revisionism, as if the memory of Infoseek is being wiped out by the Hollywood giant.

Kirsch, however, appears relaxed at the turn of events, his eye, as he later reveals, on a greater prize. The least important of these, it seems to me, is his new internet venture. For Kirsch, 43, is a philantropist on a grand scale, a man who believes he can and will make a difference to the world and its myriad problems. It is a passion that borders on the pompous. Yet there is also something wonderful and naïve about such treasured aspirations.

Can Disney make a Go of Infoseek?

Tap in the URL for Infoseek and one is immediately taken to the Go.com web page. No sign of what was once one of the strongest brands on the web. What, one wonders, did Disney pay $1.6 billion for, merely to shut down a big part of the business it was buying, namely the Infoseek name and reputation.

At the start of the new millennium, Disney announced that Go.com would no longer go head-to-head with Yahoo and the other general portals. Instead, it would narrow its focus on its core strengths, namely its entertainment content and heritage. Disney executives fretted that their site lacked the distinctive characteristics of its major rivals.

The move was not altogether unexpected. Wall Street had been predicting that the so-called second tier portals Go, Lycos and Excite, would be forced to develop a vertical niche approach and cede the all-embracing portal field to AOL and Yahoo. There was therefore a broad welcome for the Disney move. However, some commentators feel that the fate of Infoseek, subsumed into a larger entity and eventually discarded, may also await the smaller portals.

The formation of Infoseek

His early memories of getting involved in business go back to high school. He remembers himself as an inquiring student, a trait that would pave the way for his later passion for electronics, mechanics and computing:

'Well, I think probably one of my unusual careers was in high school. While I was a kid who might have been working at a fast food place making $2 an hour, I was making about $35 an hour and that's when $35 was a lot of money.

'I was repairing pinball machines which is a very highly skilled job. The reason that I had learned the skills was that my Dad bought a pinball machine for the family and it was always breaking. So rather than call a pinball repair man it was just a lot faster and easier for me to learn how it worked.

'I was interested and curious about how it worked. So I became an expert in how to repair that machine and then translated those skills to being a repairer of any machine.'

One interesting facet of the Kirsch character is a desire to not only make a difference, but also to make the situation he is dealing with better. He may have wanted to make money from the pinball repair business, but it also emerges he enjoyed helping people. It is an altruistic streak that runs strongly throughout his life.

This desire to make an impact also emerged shortly after he left college and went into the corporate world. 'It's fair to say, after my first job out of college, I was also disillusioned' he remembers. I thought, oh you can have a huge impact you know, you can go into business and people will listen to you and you can make a change. But it didn't happen that way.'

This first taste of, as Kirsch calls it, 'being a small fish in a big pool,' stirred his entrepreneurial leanings. He started his first company, Mouse Systems, in 1982, followed by Frame Technology in 1986.

Flush with money from his earlier ventures Kirsch was able to take time doing the thing he loved best, solving problems with his computer. The idea of Infoseek came along in the early 1990s. Kirsch recalls:

'A friend of mine gave me a computer library on a CD Rom, it was entitled Computer Library or Computer Select, or something like that, and he said check this out, it'll change your life!

'Well, I said oh yeah, right sure! So, for a longish time I didn't use it and then one day I tried it – I ended up using it, and then I ended up using it more and more, and I thought that gee, take this information and make it available to everybody, that would be some prize.'

It was 1992, and the internet was just beginning to make it out of the universities and into the outside world. What though, I wonder, did this system of information have that stirred something in the budding entrepreneur? 'It appealed to me as a consumer. If it's something that I need I then think well gee, is there something that other people would have a similar reaction to.'

Kirsch says his previous business experience at this stage was a real help, giving him the confidence and the resources to carry through the big idea behind Infoseek. What Kirsch had in mind was to build a searching system that would drill down further than those being developed elsewhere. The interesting thing about this is that Kirsch made this decision without any detailed knowledge of the scale or technology of the other search engines:

'The quality of the searching I knew was always going to be the important differentiator for consumers. For example, if you typed in south west on Infoseek you only get South West Airlines because that's the most likely matched term. So it's not just done in terms of simply matching the words, but also figuring out the meaning of that word you are thinking of and then getting the right answer.'

It was progressive thinking by Kirsch: the internet would get bigger, although by just how much exceeded even his ambitious estimates. Still, the notion of the smart search engine was a prescient one.

>> The notion of the smart search engine was a prescient one

What was driving him at this time? Was it profit margins or was it the need to build this thing up as quickly as possible in the face of competition?

'I don't think we were driven by the competition. I think it was more the audience. We wanted to service as many people as we could with very high-quality results.'

In hindsight, I ask Kirsch, now that he has sold Infoseek to Disney, did the business achieve the potential that he thought it could or exceed it in any way?

'No, it didn't exceed it because I wanted to have a number one site so it didn't do that.'

Did he think that going to Disney was the best thing for the group?

'I think it's an interesting strategy. Only time will tell whether it was the right one or not. It certainly lowers the downside in terms of financing. Disney is going to make available the resources to ensure that it will never fail.'

He sounds disappointed, I tell him.

'Oh because it would have been nice if we were in the position that Yahoo is in today. I would be much happier, it's like playing the game and losing, nobody likes to lose.'

So why isn't he in the position of Yahoo?

'Because we made some mistakes.'

Such as?

'Hiring the wrong CEO way back – we lost a lot of ground there. And then there was changing around strategy, not moving quickly enough.'

Was that his responsibility did he think?

'I don't know if these were my mistakes because a lot of the things I said we should do we finally did do and had dramatic success in doing that. So, I don't know that any one person is to blame. Collectively we didn't do as well as we could have.'

Well, I say, I guess in your defense, you were in a market that was changing practically by the day.

He is in no mood for apologists. 'That's so, but other competitors navigated the space.'

I try suggesting timing and luck as contributing factors.

'All certain combinations of factors can help towards your destiny. If you have six people in a race, one person is going to end up winning the race and someone's going to end up being the sixth person. That's a fact of life, everybody's trying to be number one. But the facts are that some people are going to end sixth or fifth and some people are going to end up first and some second, and often the distinction between the two may be very small, but it's still there.'

Future plans for Kirsch

Picking over the coals of Infoseek draws a certain reticence from Kirsch. I ask what kind of business leader he think he is.

He pauses, 'technical vision and some marketing and sales.'

Is he a good motivator?

'I think so.'

I switch tack to discuss his latest venture. Obviously, his bittersweet experience at Infoseek hadn't weakened his entrepreneurial resolve?

'No! I'm working like crazy. I was up until one o'clock in the morning on the computer. Then I get up at seven o'clock. So I'm getting a lot less sleep now than I used to.'

Kirsch is using some of the tens of millions of dollars he made from the Infoseek sale to fund his new venture. It is an internet infrastructure business that will help in the building of websites – 'whether it's e-commerce websites or just intra-internet,' says Kirsch enthusiastically.

'Say for example, you wanted to link with Amazon.com and you wanted to build more applications on top of that, you could use our software. If you wanted to build an intranet and you wanted to have various applications from budgeting to employee directory, to something to help manage the price development process, you might use our software.

'Typically we would licence the software to our customers who would run it at their own facility using an ASP (application service provider) to host it.'

When we met, the new company was called Abaca, but has since changed its name to Propel.com. Its website, at the time of writing, is a two-page appeal for résumés from prospective employees.

It all sounds like hard work. Especially for a very rich man like Steve Kirsch. Why bother?

'Bill Gates is wealthy too,' he retorts, and then more enthusiatically: 'For fun. Because I enjoy it, and want to make a difference. I mean you can't believe how bad things are. You look at the world and you look at the frustrations that we had at Infoseek – we had to build our own tools because there weren't any tools that were reliable and scalable.

'We spent an enormous amount of money to build that and it doesn't need to be that way. So having been through that frustration, you don't want others to have to go through that, especially if you have a better idea. You know, you go, "Gosh I know how to use that a lot better! I don't know why somebody doesn't do this." '

Kirsch's other passions are his family – he has a wife and two young children – and philanthropy. Given his burning desire to make a difference in the world of technology, this should come as little surprise. He explains:

'Well, we had to fix some things that we could do in our spare time. My wife goes to law school and takes care of the kids so that's a job for herself.

'So we picked about seven or so simple things that we could do to make a difference and we are pursuing those. It's some easy stuff like, the first one was saving the world, curing all major diseases, reforming politics, three or four others in a lifetime. 'It's all the tough stuff like they do on talk shows.'

Kirsch continues with a grin, 'Maybe I should tackle bad website designs. Or maybe I'll look at eliminating unsolicited e-mails and faxes – making that illegal – as well as banning all handguns.'

And does he simply throw money at these various 'simple things?'

'No, through spending time with people, or organizing people at my foundation, getting personally involved. For example, I'm meeting with the Mayor of San José next week to talk about getting free parking for electric vehicles at the San José airport.

'I'm working with someone at my foundation about getting an initiative on the ballot to tax the petrol car and pass on that tax to people who drive electric vehicles.'

I suddenly remember seeing in the parking lot a huge electric battery recharger and a car plugged in to it. 'Yes, that's mine,' he says proudly. 'As far as saving the world, you do that through one key person at a time. So we're working on Tom Campbell right now who's against ratification of the nuclear test ban treaty. I was in a discussion with him and pointed out the errors of his argument and haven't heard back from him since.'

I tell Kirsch his idealism is admirable.

He sighs. 'The problem is that there's too many of these things. If you just picked one of these – saving the world, for example – you could spend your life doing that.'

At least he's doing something.

He responds more brightly. 'For electric vehicles I got legislation passed in California so you can drive your electric vehicle on the freeway. That was something that other people were working on as well but I definitely spent hundreds of hours and took many trips to Sacramento and wrote up lots of documents and spent a lot of time on it and got it past the Governor.'

After we meet, I spend some time on the Steven and Michelle Kirsch Foundation website. I also visit – because it is conveniently linked from the charity – Kirsch's own site, and get the first hint of the size of this man's ego.

The foundation site tells us that the husband and wife philanthropists maintain a $75 million fund at the community foundation of Silicon Valley, a Californian philanthropy group. We are also informed that the two wealthy benefactors donated $5.7 million in 1998 to a variety of other good causes, and that something call the National Society for Fund Raising Executives' Silicon Valley chapter had named them 'Outstanding Philanthropists' for 1999.

The detailed site gives guidance on why it's good to give, why it's good to let everyone know that you've given and what areas the Kirschs are particularly interested in. In one amusing anecdote, Kirsch has published the e-mail correspondence he has had with a dying biotech billionaire trying to convince him to give away some of his cash before he dies. The conversation reads like one of those you have with someone who's life is wrapped around the detail of their existence, which is also probably one of the reasons they are billionaires in the first place.

On Kirsch's home page, we are told that his new venture, Propel, recently received funding from former Netscape executive Marc Andreesen. He apparently provided this after inquiring of Kirsch what it is Propel is going to do, to which Kirsch wrote a mysterious four-word answer. It was not, he informs us, 'This will make money.'

Elsewhere on the site there is an enormous amount of information about the man, his millions and his life. We learn, for example, that the Kirschs have donated money to research on hair loss. They are also involved in, and have provided funding for, an organization seeking to predict when a meteor will crash to the earth. In addition, there are long tracts on Steve Kirsch's favorite household appliances, gadgets and vehicles.

It all adds up to a rather unhealthy overexposure of a nerd who obviously means well, but who would perhaps be better advised to focus more on running his business interests. How, one wonders, did he find the time to help run Infoseek in the middle of all this do-gooding and self-promotion? To which he would doubtlessly reply that the hundreds of millions of dollars he has earned as an entrepreneur are all the testament he needs.

My philosophy is t
be very committed to
doing the right things fo
the customers and tryir
lots of things

Rod Schrock
AltaVista

From big business to net start-up

I'm hyper-aggressive, very customer-orientated and also very experimental. It's important to get in and understand what the market is about and experiment, try things that you think are new and different and users might like. If they like them fine, you build on top of them, if not you move on very quickly. But my philosophy is to be very committed to doing the right things for the customers and trying lots of things. If they don't succeed, I'm quick in recognizing that and moving on. It's about being willing to be wrong. You have to be very confident in trying things and admitting when they don't work. Many people try things and when they don't work they try to rationalize it, try to justify and build on it whereas my philosophy is more, 'That didn't work let's move on and learn something from that.'

Introduction

When Rod Schrock, then a high-flying executive for Compaq Computer, was asked what the company should do with its AltaVista internet portal, he told them to sell it to Yahoo. It was perhaps not the most auspicious start to his internet career, but in early 1999 he was handed the job anyway of improving AltaVista's fortunes.

The company was sitting snugly – far too snugly for most observers – in the second tier of search engines, alongside Lycos, Snap.com, Go and Excite@Home. It was Schrock's task to try and differentiate AltaVista from its rivals – and, if he could, elevate the group to the status of the market giants, America Online, Yahoo and MSN.

One year into the job and the obstacles to achieving this seem to be growing larger every day. A recent report from Forrester, the US research group, predicts that internet advertising will migrate away from the portal sites

>> It was Schrock's task to try and differentiate
AltaVista from its rivals

towards more niche destinations. Thus, the report believes, banks will increasingly prefer to advertise with specific financial service sites, car manufacturers with auto hubs and airlines with specific travel sites.

At the same time, the Big Three portals are pulling away. They currently account for 15 percent of web traffic and 45 percent of advertising; in

5 ways...

Rod Schrock
broke the
rules

1   Recommended AltaVista be sold before taking on the job of CEO.

2   Ratcheted up recruitment – and losses – without a defined strategy.

3   Struck a myriad alliances and introduced new services in order to
    differentiate AltaVista.

4   Became the first of the second tier portals to outline a niche service.

5   Continues to believe that consolidation is the key to success.

contrast, figures for the second tier are 5 and 10 percent respectively. Forrester forecasts that the second tier portal audience share will drop to just 1 percent by 2004. Given the market trends, few analysts would disagree with that prediction.

The portal model emerged around 1997 as a means for the internet search engine groups to move more quickly to profitability. With millions of web users entering the internet through their sites, the search engines realized that if they could hold on to this traffic for as long as possible, they would be able to increase rates to advertisers as well as realize e-commerce revenues.

A spending spree followed, which continues to this day, with the portal groups seeking to acquire sites and companies that would widen the wealth of services they offered to visitors. Thus financial services, news services, community sites and e-commerce opportunities became key battlegrounds, with the portals inking deals with a variety of on- and off-line groups. Unfortunately, the myriad different offerings have all but canceled out any differentiation between the portals, with the result that the bigger sites have continued to pull away from their smaller rivals.

However, there are plenty of suggestions – from Wall Street to venture capitalists to market commentators – about what the likes of AltaVista and Excite should do about their predicament. Wall Street's favored endgame is an orgy of mergers, which would see the smaller portal groups linking up with media companies anxious to share their content with the internet companies' audience reach – e.g. AOL and Time Warner.

Go, the Disney subsidiary, for one is not waiting for any advice. It has already signalled that it intends to retreat from the bruising, and costly, battle to be a general-purpose web gateway. It intends to reinvent itself as an entertainment portal, emphasizing its Disney heritage and distinctive content.

So too AltaVista. Schrock has also moved to reposition his company, focussing on financial services, e-commerce and search. The strategy involves giving away the source code for its search engine and paying websites that successfully refer people to AltaVista.

As part of its new AltaVista Affiliate Network, the portal will allow websites to offer its services, such as search, stock quotes and language translation, free of charge. In addition, AltaVista will pay the sites three cents for every click-through. Schrock estimates that some 10 000 sites will be in the scheme within the first month. 'We are not trying to be a general-purpose portal,' he said on announcing the initiative. 'We want to be world class in a few areas.'

Joining AltaVista

Schrock, 41, is by no means a typical entrepreneur – if indeed there is such a thing. There was no great idea, no opportunistic jump, and no futuristic zeal. He is in short, a company man. Yet he for one is not surprised to find himself running an internet business. Indeed, he would contend that the entrepreneurial spirit runs deep, and it was merely a question of time before he got to prove his credentials.

Schrock came from a moderately wealthy business family. In his youth, he worked part-time in his father's grocery store, where he says he learned the art of business, making money and the value of success. One lesson he remembers from his childhood has stuck with him:

'My dad had a great saying. One thing about him was he was very competitive, very determined to succeed. When I was about 11 or 12 years old, I used to play basketball and I was playing with my uncle, and my dad was playing with my brother.

'Up until that time I could never beat my dad at anything, but we started playing basketball and we got ahead by a couple of points and I got so excited I yelled out "We are winning" – and my dad immediately grabbed the ball, stopped the whole game and said "You're not winning, you're ahead, you haven't won until the game's over!" And that lasted with me forever.'

Schrock's business career began in classic style – a degree from Harvard, which followed brief spells working for IBM and Apple. He joined Compaq after graduating, a move he believes was a brave one:

'Compaq you have to understand was very entrepreneurial between 1982 and 1986 during its formative years. You have to realize their number one challenge was: how was IBM not going to put them out of business that quarter!

'IBM was a formidable competitor and at that point in time the PC industry didn't have the standards that it has today. So it was quite a risk to go and work for Compaq in those days. In fact when I left business school, friends said, boy, you're taking a big risk going there.'

The ambitious young graduate rose to manage various parts of the Compaq organization over the next 12 years. 'My time at Compaq was really about running new businesses, or being put in charge of those areas that weren't performing well and trying to sort them out,' Schrock says. Part of this experience involved managing Compaq's consumer division, to which AltaVista was attached when Compaq acquired Digital Equipment in 1998. It was to be a fortuitous move.

Schrock believes it was an advantage running businesses within a business, allowing him the financial freedom that perhaps would have constrained him in less benevolent situations:

'Yes, it did help. It is very similar frankly to the internet space today because the capital markets are supporting you and the venture capital is supporting you without you having to worry about making money immediately.

'But yes, there was an advantage (being within a large organization) because we started two major businesses – the whole network server business using PC technology and then going to the actual consumer market selling PCs to people in their homes. In both cases we lost significant amounts of money for two to three years before we turned them around to profitability.'

However, he denies that the pressure to succeed is any less in a corporate situation, such as Compaq, compared to a start-up:

'Yes, a big company gives you breathing space you may not have otherwise. But you have to realize that when you are in a large corporation where they are used to success – you know they make money every quarter – you are somewhat of a pariah if you are in a group that is not making much money. So you have to be very determined, you have to be willing to survive in that type of environment.'

Schrock says his reaction to being offered the AltaVista job, at the beginning of 1999, was one of excitement. He saw it as a chance to prove himself in the public as well as the corporate arena:

'My view was this was my third turn at writing a success story. I had done this twice before within Compaq, but this one was certainly more visible because when you are in a corporate environment you are well known within the company and with the people that you interface with. But this was a chance to become well known with the public at large and an opportunity to demonstrate a capability on the public stage rather than in a private way.'

Schrock was not angling for the AltaVista job. Although the internet intrigued him, and there was little doubting the enormous challenge the subsidiary posed, he was enjoying running the business he had built up:

'I was not lobbying for the job. I was running a $5 billion successful consumer PC business. We were number one in markets here and abroad, and, almost by accident, AltaVista is put inside my group.

'Imagine you are running a 5 billion dollar business and they put a little 10 million dollar internet company inside? You know you have to have a lot of strength and character and know what the future is all about to justify spending a lot of time on the 10 million dollar piece rather than the 4.99 billion dollar piece!'

But spend time on it he did:

'I was asked to figure out what to do with AltaVista. I actually went to a board meeting and recommended that we form a strategic partnership with Yahoo in which case we would put money in AltaVista. I was rejected at that board meeting and right after that meeting the chairman of the board, Ben Rosen, and CEO, Eckhard Pfeifer, basically got me in a room and said we want to unlock the value of AltaVista. We are not going to sell it and therefore we want you to run the company – that was how it got started.'

But what qualifications did Schrock think he had to run an internet business? After all, Compaq was not renowned for its web strategy or presence.

'Well, we had championed internet PCs, and we had championed internet connectivity – that's the reason why people buy home PCs and get onto the internet. They use Compaq PCs – that's how I was qualified to run an internet company.'

Schrock's business strategy for AltaVista

Taking over a company you have recommended would best sit as part of another organization – namely Yahoo – and being told to run with it as

1 Much of the company's development will depend on the strategy of CMGI, AltaVista's owner.

2 AltaVista probably has the weakest brand of the second line portals.

3 Building visibility is a crucial test.

4 Forging an alliance, partnership or merger with a media company would bring enormous benefits.

5 Continuing to differentiate the AltaVista service and maintaining the momentum the new management has injected.

5 hurdles...

for Rod Schrock and AltaVista

an independent company must be among the most challenging of managerial tasks. Schrock's answer was to reposition AltaVista, to try and differentiate the group – a task he continues to wrestle with:

'Initially, we decided to aim for a clear top four global position. We are about number six or number seven globally now. In doing so, we were moving away from the other technology companies to some extent, because we were saying that we are still going to be an excellent search engine – but that we are going to be a new media company, a new media commerce company if you will. And we are going to define our competition as Yahoo and other companies, but really we would zero in on Yahoo as our primary competition.

'When we made that announcement we had 55 engineers on the West Coast and myself and I think in that same month Yahoo hired their one thousandth employee. So from my perspective it would take a Herculean effort to put AltaVista in a position of being able to compete long term successfully and independently with Yahoo.

'That was my perspective then. Has it changed? I don't know to be honest with you, the jury is still out. I think that we have made a number of good moves, we have over 650 employees, we are probably one or two major acquisitions away from propelling ourselves in the top five position.

'But we have one additional major advantage and that is CMGI has acquired the majority ownership in AltaVista, and that combination probably puts us in a position where long term perhaps we could be a major leader.'

Here Schrock is undoubtedly right. CMGI, headed by David Wetherell, has become one of the most important players in the internet market, making shrewd strategic investments in a wide range of companies. Initially this was merely a venture capital operation. However, the company has developed into an incubator, helping its companies with management and introductions. It has also announced plans to build a network of internet companies that will interact with each other. CMGI is by far the best asset AltaVista has.

>> CMGI is by far the best asset AltaVista has

Has anything changed with the ownership of CMGI in terms of strategy? 'If anything we are more aggressive,' says Schrock. 'We have the capital backing from CMGI to continue and invest in the acquisitions and operating expenses to build AltaVisa. I think it's been a very strong, positive situation for us because CMGI is known as a savvy internet development company because they develop new companies to be successful.' He is also appreciative of the CMGI management style:

'I would characterize them as very actively interested supporters of AltaVista. But they are not by any means hands-on micro managers. Dave Wetherell and I participate in a staff meeting once a week, he and I trade e-mails on a daily basis and talk maybe two or three times a week, But it's not like they have an active management role or anything like that. I think they are fairly confident with the track we are on, and they are just trying to be very supportive with what we do.

'CMGI is a unique company. I believe they are the corporate model of the future, because they have venture capital funds and they fund new things, and they also continue to scan the landscape of what is going on. But they also independently encourage individual entities within their companies to be publicly traded, so people have their own motivation to be successful.'

Among the acquisitions Schrock has made are: e-commerce company shopping.com; personalized portal company Zip2; search focus company I-Atlas; and finance community concern RagingBull.com. He still needs other acquisitions, however:

'We still have to cement a top four or top five e-commerce network position. Today our e-commerce effort is kind of top 15 in terms of visitors, but it's not top ten like AltaVista search, so that's an area that we have to continue strengthening. Then we have to strengthen probably our overall community capabilities beyond just message boards which is what Raging Bull is all about.'

Schrock inherited a fairly disillusioned workforce:

'When I took over at AltaVista, they had had maybe two or three or four aborted attempts to become an independent company. It was a small, highly successful internet company for one function, searching the internet, trapped within this 70 000 employee environment and with all this digital equipment.

'They also had this background of, on numerous occasions, trying to develop strategies aimed at becoming an independent company and all of those were wrong, and their leadership they put in place failed to achieve that. So I would say the employee base was skeptical and also a little bit disillusioned.'

Thus, in addition to figuring out how to revamp the company's strategy, Schrock was also faced with the task of motivating the workforce: 'We had to develop a strategy, we had to reinvigorate the employee base, and we had to hire – 400 employees in 10 months. Yes, it's been challenging.' Naturally, none of this has come cheap:

'The investment in AltaVista is in the billions of dollars. We spent almost $800 million on acquisitions and then we are investing $125 million on advertising, branding and a marketing campaign. We spent over $100 million on 140 mini computer systems in the last two months in order to handle increased traffic – we now have a large enough data center to store an entire duplicate copy of the internet. This is probably the largest investment in information systems of anyone on the internet.'

Although our meeting took place some weeks before the announcement of the AltaVista Affiliates Network, Schrock was already expounding the virtues of such a system – and how it would differentiate the group from the other portals:

'Well, to us a network is a network of interesting sites and services. Some of them will stay as stand-alone, single-theme sites – shopping.com for example is an e-commerce site, whereas RagingBull.com is a financial community interest site and so forth. But a network basically means you take a network of sites and integrate them very tightly to allow people to navigate across the internet through your network.

'A portal is more….

Actually portal I'm not sure has much of a definition, it gets used by everybody. Everybody sets their site up as a portal today, there are millions of portal sites out there right now, so it's kind of lost its definition or never really achieved its definition.'

Another part of the Schrock strategy is to build on AltaVista's overseas strengths, which account for 60 percent of its traffic: 'We really want to be a top four global player and building a global network is part of that. We are thinking and approaching this at a global level because it's a fact that we are stronger outside the US. For example, we are number two in traffic in the UK and Sweden, number four in France, number two in Italy.'

Possible future partnerships

Despite his success, Schrock maintains a beady eye on prospective alliances. The cross-holdings of CMGI in AltaVista and rival search engine Lycos have prompted much speculation among investors and analysts that a merger could be on the cards. Indeed, Morgan Stanley, the US investment bank and one of AltaVista's advisers, are reported to have said that bringing the two companies together would create a web dream team. Schrock does not baulk at the thought:

'We have discussed it. I am a supporter as I said (of partnerships and alliances). We are a new media company where our brand is our most differentiating feature to our audience and, as you know, no single brand can capture an entire audience. It's very difficult for a single brand to do

>> Despite his success, Schrock maintains a beady eye on prospective alliances

that, so I am actually a fan of multiple brands working together to capture the widest possible audience. If it (a merger) were to occur with Lycos you know I would be in support of it but I really think that it's up to Lycos to determine what to do.'

'I think Lycos is probably number four domestically and top five globally. I think AltaVista is number ten domestically, probably top six or top seven globally. If you want to propel yourself into the number two position globally you have to make a big move similar to that.'

Bob Davis is one of the major obstacles. The CEO of Lycos has declared his intention to remain independent, particularly after a bruising battle to convince shareholders of the merits of a merger with USA Networks. The deal collapsed after fearful investors refused to back it, anxious over the price USA Networks was valuing Lycos at. In the process, relations between Davis and CMGI's Wetherell were said to have suffered.

Wetherell initially supported the deal, but withdrew CMGI's support as the Lycos price drifted away. CMGI retains a 16 percent interest in Lycos.

With an IPO set for 2000, Schrock remains optimistic about AltaVista even if it does not feature in any further consolidation in the portal market:

'I am of the opinion by the way that this space is so large that you don't have to be number one or one of the top two or three largest sites in the world to be successful. I just don't think that's the requirement, although you do have to achieve scale and the bigger the scale the more successful you are. But being one of the top ten internet companies, if you maintain that position for 20 years you are going to be one of the top ten companies in the world.'

It didn't really matter what we did, we just wanted to be working together. And not work for anyone else

10

Joe Kraus
Excite

Passion and commitment
to a business ideal

Introduction

Every second Thursday, six young men meet for dinner in Silicon Valley. They are multimillionaires, all under 30 and at the hub of the internet revolution.

Joe Kraus, Graham Spencer, Martin Rheinfield, Ben Lutch, Mark VanHaren and Ryan McIntyre are the founders of Excite, one of the best-known internet search engine groups. Only Kraus and Spencer remain with the company today, the others are described by their publicist as 'freelance entrepreneurs', involved in funding and managing a variety of internet projects. Yet the story of how the six Californian college friends decided to start a company – any company – together is one to stir the blood of any prospective internet entrepreneur.

The formation of Excite

The year is 1993, the internet is in its infancy, venture capital is hard to come by and the spirit of risk and adventure hardly figures on investors' radar screens. For Joe Kraus, it is a defining moment. Unlike his colleagues, he is a political scientist, while they are technologists. They have the bright technical know-how, he brings... well, it's not exactly clear what he brings, but he's happy to be there for the ride.

Kraus says he never had any interest in business until he went to Stanford University, the famous Californian college that has spawned a myriad net ventures. Once there, he was struck by the heady atmosphere of entrepreneurism and the general clamor for success:

'I think college was very formative. Stanford has an amazing position as a university in the sense that it's in the heart of Silicon valley. You're constantly introduced to role models who have made it.

'In Silicon Valley, through Stanford, you're given a sense that the coolest thing to be doing is to be starting your own company, or working for a very small company.

'If you go to other parts of the US, the middle of Ohio for example, and you say, I'm going to start my own company, or work with five or six other people in a very small company, you are looked at as what's wrong with you? What happened, you're not good enough to get a job with a big firm?

'And I credit Stanford, by showing role models in Silicon Valley, with bringing out and encouraging a lot of the entrepreneurial tendencies.'

Kraus's early business experience started during the summer vacations. Even here, in part-time work just to make some extra cash, his desire to be self-employed was strong:

'I didn't even want to work for anybody else in the summers. So a friend of mine and I started a design T-shirt company in Los Angeles where I had grown up. And that was definitely the first taste of – wow, it's good not to work for anyone else!

'I had friends who were working 9–5 jobs for $5 an hour, whereas my friend and I were working longer hours but the ones we wanted. It was flexible time and we were earning a lot more than $5 an hour, and that was the first experience of – wow, it's actually great not to have a boss.

'More important than that, we were completely determining our own ability to succeed – we succeeded or failed based on nothing more than our ability to do the job effectively, and that becomes very addictive.'

That was not the only influence on the young Kraus's ambitions. A negative experience while he was still a high school student also left its mark:

'My parents returned home from an auction and they said they'd bought me something – a summer job! This was in my senior year at high school and I said what, you've bought me a job? And they said, yeah it's in an architectural and engineering firm. I said this is terrible, I don't want this!

'But I went to work for this firm and my job was duplicating microfiche, and I don't know if you have been around microfiche or duplicated microfiche, but it's a miserable process.

'It involves taking a piece of film and the original microfiche and exposing it to ultra violet light. So you get a sunburn right there, and then you put it in the development tray which sprays ammonia on it which chokes you. I did this for six weeks, working with three 65-year-old women. I went bananas, it was the end of me. I basically said to myself: I am never ever, ever doing this again.

'In many ways it was a defining moment in the sense that I said, I cannot do this, and ended up quitting and working in a grocery store as a bag packer. And my parents at that point realized, well, perhaps Joe's not cut out for the microfiche role.'

But Kraus has nothing but praise for his family after that:

'When I was selling T-shirts, I think my parents probably thought, oh boy now we are going to have to support him over the summer.

'But then they saw me actually pulling down some reasonable contracts and making a go of it and they were very supportive. It was the same way when we started Excite, they were really nervous at first, but once it started getting some momentum, they were great.'

The T-shirt business certainly sharpened Kraus's business technique. He recalls:

'There were four major T-shirt printing houses in Los Angeles and all of them that we visited would say, your order is too small. So I said, just humor us and take us on a tour of your facility.

5 ways...

Joe Kraus
broke the
rules

1   As the only non-technologist among the founders, Kraus could have been intimidated into taking a subordinate role. He was not.

2   Recognized early on the need for good vibrant marketing – a factor that transformed Excite into one of the most exciting brands on the net.

3   His and his colleagues' honesty in admitting that they did not know how to make money from their venture was more than brave, it bordered on the suicidal. But it worked.

4   Admitting also that they needed senior experienced management to help them. Brave and boring but essential.

5   Merging with @Home. The jury's still out, but it was the first deal of its kind – marrying broadband cable with net content.

'Here we'd meet the foreman, who was the person who ran all the machines – and invariably had an operation in the backyard where he would be making T-shirts at a fraction of the cost of what the T-shirt house was.

'So we would go into these big manufacturing plants and meet the foreman and do business on the side out of their backyards and beat everyone's prices as a result.'

Excite was born in a Mexican food bar called Roseda's. I ask Kraus what the internet buzz was like at that time:

'Well remember when we got together at Roseda's, in February 1993, none of us had seen the web. We had all been playing with the internet for four years while we were at school, but it was primarily through very primitive text interfaces, using text-based e-mail and things like that.

'So we had no idea the internet was going to be the thing. The only conclusion we came to was that more information was going to be made available electronically and it needed better tools for searching through it. That was our only insight.'

The concept of starting a company around a group of individuals, rather than a concept or idea, still strikes Kraus as almost unique:

'It didn't really matter what we did, we just wanted to be working together. And not work for anybody else – that was the other aspect of it. So, one day at Roseda's, we each came with different business ideas. Unfortunately, they all sucked. They were things like applications for the Newton (Apple's hand-held computer), remember the Newton? Yeah a really good idea!

>> Excite was born in a Mexican food bar called Roseda's

'Translation software, which never goes anywhere. And it was when we were depressed at the end of this meal, Graham said, "Let's build tools for searching through large databases – there's going to be more and more information around". '

It was the start of Excite. By the summer of 1994, the team had built a working demo of the technology behind the fledgling search engine. Kraus recalls:

'We needed to put an interface on it and I remember Graham saying we could put one on a programme called Supercard, which you will remember if you were a Mac user. Or, we could do it in this new thing called mosaic and it's on this thing called the web.

'So, I said let's try it on the web. So we built a web-based interface on our technology, not because we knew it was the future and not because we knew it was going to be huge, but because it was convenient. It looked like there was an emerging standard that was going on and we suddenly got associated with being a web company as a result of that.'

Kraus feigns amnesia as to what was the business idea he proposed at the meeting, 'I think it was something for lawyers or something like that. Thank god, I've decided to completely erase that from my mind,' he laughs.

Kraus's particular role in Excite

His position as the non-technologist pushed Kraus into the job of marketing and selling the Excite idea. In fact, he earned the nickname 'phoneboy' – his main task while his friends were developing the software being to get on the phone to bankers, investors, the coffee shop, whoever. He explains:

'The disadvantage I probably felt at the time was that I had no programming experience. But the thing that I knew I did have was an ability to talk to people and an ability to communicate. So when all this programming was going on, I felt that I was contributing uniquely because my job was very different to the rest of the jobs in the venture.'

>> A fresh approach to marketing has helped turn
      Excite into one of the best brands on the web

'I would read the newspaper every morning, scouring it for names that would be interested in what we were building. I would cold-call them, just to get a phone call in to them, describe what we were doing and convince them that it was the best thing on earth.'

Kraus admits:

'It was hard to feel like you are being productive because you are not writing the lines of code and making this new thing work.

'But I was contributing in a different way and it takes longer for that contribution to pay off, but ultimately it does. You build relationships and we ultimately and successfully raised the money.'

Kraus is being over-modest. Behind the still youthful features – he is after all still only 28 – you sense there lurks a steely ambition. Friend or no friend, he has proved himself a tenacious worker, bringing a fresh approach to marketing that has helped turn Excite into one of the best brands on the web. Indeed, a story he tells from the early Excite days illustrates well his determination, as well as an astonishing self-confidence:

Kraus on the nostalgia of the start-up

I think the funny part is, I look back on those days in the garage as really exciting. But they are only exciting because they led to an outcome which is today. I think if we were still in the garage six years later, I think we would be hating life, and that would be really tough. Sure there's a nostalgia about this – the way we were as a small company, but I think that in reality it was an amazingly stressful and uncertain time.

'We were working out of a garage in summer 1993. I decided to take a part-time job to help get by, but the ones that paid the best were the technical jobs. What does a political science major in a part-time job do? Not a lot! So I decided to get a programming job, even though I would have to fake my way into it.

'A friend of mine worked in a database company and he said that he had some contract positions for some engineers, but you needed C++ programming experience. So, I thought, I can do this, it pays $20 an hour. I can afford to be half time there and then I can afford to work in the garage.

'They called me the next day and said the budget's been cut for the position and we really don't have it open anymore! Darn! So, I called them the next day and said I will make you a deal, hire me at $5 an hour, and give me this job and in three months at $20 an hour.

'And they said ok we'll take it. So I don't know if they knew I was a fake or whether the budget really got cut, but I started working there at $5 an hour in a technical programming position. It was hysterical because the first day I arrived my boss sat me down at the computer and he goes 'do XYZ' and I just froze. I had no idea how to do what he was asking me to do.

'I was sitting there with my hands on the computer and he was telling me exactly what to type and I felt so exposed in my inability. But in those kind of situations, you learn very quickly, and I survived.'

So, ironically, the one member of the team who could not program was working part-time to help support the new venture… as a programmer, albeit a basic one.

Funding the 'big idea'

Being so heavily weighted in the technical department led the friends to decide early on that it would be managerial experience as well as funding that would be an essential part of their success:

'I think an important thing that all entrepreneurs have to go through, an important question to ask, is if it's more important to be successful than be in control and we answered the question from day one.

'That meant that we needed to hire adult supervision and additional management. Another thing is that when you are coming out of college, you don't know much about business – you only have perceptions of what other people have taught you and what other role models look like. And by definition, those start-ups that were successful were those that raised money from venture capitalists.

'We were actively begging them to invest and so by the time they came in it was a major milestone.'

I'm stuck by the notion of these two college kids – one in shorts and T-shirts – showing up in the Sandhill Road, home of the Valley's big VCs, and selling the Excite story.

'We had talked to several venture capitalists, well 15 in all, who saw a demonstration of our technology. All of them said that it was really cool. Then their first question after a demonstration was always: How do you make money?

'And our answer was: We don't know, we figured you could help us out with that. We know the technology and we know where this industry's going, we think the net's going to be big and we figured you can help us figure out how to make money from it!

'Well, as you can imagine, most venture capitalists don't like that proposition. In fact they shut down most of the conversations, in fact all of the conversations, very quickly.

'So we got known in the Valley as a bunch of smart kids with really neat stuff, that there was something going on there, but who had no idea how we were going to make money from it.

'That was until we met Vinod Khosla from Kleiner Perkins. He sat back after five minutes of seeing us, and didn't ask how we were going to make money. He asked can you search big technology databases, is it scalable?

'And that was such a refreshing question! We said: "Oh that's interesting, we don't know because we can't afford a hard drive that's big enough to test." So Vinod gets on his cell phone and calls his assistant and within ten minutes buys us this $6000 hard drive!

'When you meet a person like that, who is trying to figure out how to take this thing and make it even bigger than you can possibly imagine, and they are not saying "gimme, gimme gimme," they are saying "how do we take this thing and go with it?" You feel like you are working with a real partner.

'So you are willing in those cases to say, well this person's out to help me be successful and help the company be successful and so yeah you give up a lot of equity. But at the same time you know that it is more important to be successful than in control – it wasn't a situation we were worried about.

'We weren't going to fight for control. It was a situation where we had definite visions of where it was going to go, but we were flexible, we knew that it was going to require us to take different jobs, to contribute in different ways in order to be successful.'

What would have happened, I wonder, if the venture capitalists had come in and said that we like these technology guys but the political scientist, what's he in this for?

'It would have been a bummer, It's funny because I was the guy, along with with Graham Spencer, pitching – he and I would be the main tag team that would go into all these different venture capital meetings and do the dog and pony demonstrations of, hey here's what we have going. We worked really well together.

'I would dress in a suit, Graham would have T-shirt and shorts on. It wasn't on purpose, that was just the way that we both thought it appropriate to dress. It turns out it was also in the Silicon Valley classic ideal of the brilliant technologist in T-shirt and shorts! Even in the most important meetings, he was in a T-shirt and shorts – he did step up to jeans at one point, which was good.'

'We had a rapport, we had a style that worked. I was the guy who was selling and Graham didn't speak much, but everything he said was so incredible and so golden that it worked.

'It was one of those things where I was the guy who was preaching religion and selling and just looking into people's eyes and saying how can you miss this opportunity?

'And Graham would provide the credibility. So to answer your question, there was never a fear for my own part because I felt like we were all a team. You have to realize that when you have never seen anything about what can go wrong or right in venture capital, you assume it's going to work.

'Maybe I'm just fundamentally optimistic, but it was a situation where I never contemplated they would do this without me being involved. It just felt like if a venture capitalist was going to invest, our presumption was they were going to because they feel like you're signing up with a person who not only is going to give you money but is going to help you all the way through.

'We got very lucky in that way. And yeah it was tough giving up equity. Plus, the other thing is that in the Valley, once you get one offer from a venture capitalist suddenly everybody who said no to you before says we didn't really mean no, what we meant was yes.'

1 Delivering on the @Home deal. The bottom line still sags through huge marketing bills. The market awaits the big breakthrough in terms of increasing visitors and usage.

2 Developing new and original content to differentiate Excite from the other portals.

3 Building on the merger to bring in other services, such as more extensive distribution.

4 Cementing the management team after recent upheavals.

5 Drop the @Home name and focus on building the stronger Excite brand across a variety of media.

5 hurdles...

for Joe Kraus and Excite

Were those offers more attractive than Kleiner Perkins?

'Sure. Once you get the Kleiner stamp, suddenly a lot of people are interested. We had offers that were far less dilutive, but we decided not to take them because we thought our biggest chances of being successful were to partner with the people who seem to get it, and seem to understand how to make it bigger.

'So yes they certainly got a lot of equity but they were offering so much in return besides money which we thought was valuable. It wasn't that is was softball but it was certainly an easier pitch to take.'

George Bell becomes CEO

The 'adult supervision' that was brought into Excite came in the form of George Bell. What was it about him that attracted Kraus and his colleagues?

'Well we looked for a CEO for nine months, and we realized that the most important thing we needed was culture fit. You can hire someone with a great CV, but if they don't fit within the team and they don't fit within the culture... companies are very much like people, they have antibodies.'

And what is the Excite culture exactly?

'I would say it's very energetic, open, smart, wants to win more than anything else, wants to think big, very action-orientated. Those would be the things that really define the culture.'

George Bell certainly had these characteristics, Kraus recalls:

'When we met George, we had met a lot of CEO candidates. He was the last candidate we actually saw and, if you must know, we made offers to two other candidates before George, who turned us down – thank goodness!

'The thing we loved about George was his optimism. Remember back in '95 it wasn't clear the internet was going to be big. People from the East Coast and bigger companies didn't want to come out to Silicon Valley and go to a little start-up that was hugely risky and which could be disastrous for their careers if it didn't work.

'The environment was very different from what it is today and you would have to beg most interview candidates and really sell them the story. But George was one of these guys who you knew thought, 'OK I sort of get what's happening here, let me get into the details, let me get into the business, let's figure this out.'

'He just had an energy level, a willingness to learn. For example, if back then you wanted to start a new music label, what did you do? You went out and hired people that have built music labels in the past. Well in '95 if you wanted to build a successful internet company you didn't go out and find successful internet executives, because there weren't any.

'You had to create it from the ground up, which meant you had to build an amalgamation of skills. We brought people from publishing, the video game industry, software and credit card companies and consumer good companies, and put them all together.

'But it also meant that while people needed to bring experience, you needed to make sure they could learn new things and could do things differently, because internet groups didn't operate the way these other companies operated. You move much faster, you take much bigger risks, you bet the company all the time.'

Necessary changes for the future

Kraus stepped aside when Bell arrived and moved into business development. This enabled him, and some of the other Excite directors, to concentrate on strategy, while Bell focussed on operational issues. However, it eventually became apparent that the business needed to partner with a distributor if it was to achieve its potential. This came in the form of cable group @Home, which acquired Excite for $6.7 billion in early 1999.

'Excite's business really has three components,' explains Kraus:

'We are about attracting as many consumers as possible, we are about retaining those consumers, and we are about monetarizing that audience.

'Excite has always been very good at retaining our audience and very good at making money from the people that we have. The weakest link in our chain has always been attracting new users. We have always paid money for distribution, to Netscape or Microsoft, or put money into advertising. But we always found our weakest link was getting new consumers.

'So we basically had media but very little distribution. @Home had a lot of distribution but very little media. That made a perfect marriage because we knew we needed to combine distribution and media to be successful. So we just looked at it at a macro level and said you know what, this makes sense to combine these two.

'There was also a belief that the two groups could feed on one another. So, we had 20 million customer relationships with people in the media world, all of whom were potential subscribers to @Home and the cheapest way to market them was not to run television commercials but to send them a targeted e-mail.

'In fact, one of the biggest, if not the biggest, sources of lead and customer acquisition today is Excite consumers who receive a targeted e-mail saying why don't you sign up for @Home. It's much cheaper than running a television campaign.'

Despite the strides the company has made, Kraus still worries about the future:

'I stay awake every night thinking about our competition and being out-spent in the marketplace, or being out-marketed or losing critical deals.

'The analogy I always make is that a start-up is very much like a qualifying race in the Olympics. Every event that you run, every major milestone that you achieve, crossing the finish line in first place – you feel great about it. But you realize that all it does is qualify you for the next round with competitors that are much more competitive.

'So when we got our first round of funding from Kleiner Perkins, we woke up the next morning even more scared, because we weren't competing with people that were unfunded, we were competing against the companies that were more funded than we were!

'The interesting part is that now we are at a level where we are competing with Microsoft and AOL and some real giants, and that keeps me up at night!'

It is probably not the only thing to disturb him. The merger with @Home has not been the stuff of dreams. Confusion over what Excite@Home stands for in the marketplace, poor performances in certain areas and managerial upsets, have dogged the marriage.

The group kicked off the new millennium by shaking up its board and announcing a move into the black. It was certainly a fillip the stock price needed. The net income of $514 000 was the group's first ever profitable quarter, and followed a loss of $4.5 million on a pro forma basis for the same period a year ago. Revenue rose to $128.8 million, up from $73.3 million a year ago. However, including one-time items, the company reported a net loss of $723 million for the quarter.

Meanwhile, the company called back George Bell, who had become president of the merged group, as chief executive, leaving Tom Jermoluk, the former CEO of @Home and of the new entity, as chairman of the board. 'The company has gotten kicked around a lot in the past year as the stepchild of the cable companies and as a stepchild of regulators,' Bell told analysts. 'But guess what? The company is not a stepchild to anyone. We are the leaders in broadband today, and will be tomorrow.'

>> The merger with @Home has not been the stuff of dreams

Kraus will be hoping that Bell can allay concerns about the company's relationship with its cable partners, such as AT&T, Cox Communications and Comcast, which are both investors and board members.

A tracking stock for Excite's media assets is also planned, which should help separate the two different sides of Excite@Home – the broadband access business and the content business – thus allowing investors to track the value of each individually. It will also free the group to use its stock as an acquisition tool without diluting cable operator ownership.

For Kraus and Excite, the hope must be that the aspirations that surrounded the merger with @Home will now be realized. If not, his and his colleagues' much-vaunted gifts for blending the right cultures with entrepreneurship may be called into question.

" I didn't actually ov
a computer until a mor
before the company
started "

" We are a media
company, not a technol
company "

11

Candice Carpenter
Nancy Evans
iVillage

A different vision
of net sucess

Introduction

Candice Carpenter and Nancy Evans came into the internet out of frustration at the medium's limitations, rather than excitement at its potential. Their attitude of 'Let's make the web meaningful and useful to women's lives,' has remained the ground rule governing iVillage's development over the past four years. Today it is the biggest women's site on the web.

There are other distinctive characteristics of the two female entrepreneurs. Both were successfully established in traditional media industries prior to iVillage, Carpenter in the television and video market, Evans in publishing.

Moving into the new medium has not changed their view that success on the internet will be achieved through a combination of branding and meaningful content. Hence their decision to base themselves in the media capital of America, New York. 'We are a media company, not a technology company,' says Evans. In fact, the whole atmosphere at the group's extensive Fifth Avenue offices speaks publishing and print, rather than the high-tech spartan surrounds of many Silicon Valley start-ups.

Neither Evans, 46, nor Carpenter, 48, has a technological background. It is a fact that they see as having advantages and disadvantages – the former being that they can come at problems left-field without the knowledge of a technologist immediately saying what can and cannot be done, but on the other hand, reliant on outsiders who perhaps do not share their values.

'I didn't actually own a computer until a month before the company started,' recalls Carpenter.

'I was consulting for AOL at the time, and so I thought I'd better get one. But then I remember going on-line for the first time – it was an unbelievable trauma!

'Then I started looking around at what was on-line and my feeling was, "this thing sucks", I mean it was really not very good, it was not at all compelling.'

Surfing amid the mass of male-orientated leisure sites and computer sales destinations, Carpenter concluded they 'said nothing to me and ultimately to millions of others.' It was a frustration that led to the idea of creating something new on the web. 'Deep down, underneath all this, there was something else, a deep vibrant interaction among people,' says Carpenter.

'Nancy and I both felt that the ability to interact with one's peers, which wasn't really being done, seemed very powerful.

'It seemed more important than the pictures on the screen, which were really just a bad substitute for print at the time. So we thought, what if we could haul that conversation up and brand it in the classic sense of branding, and make it a place that stood for something, with a certain kind of focussed conversation, it would be very relevant to people's lives.'

Their site would incorporate, she says, 'all the things that are relevant to people like us – our kids, health and working lives.' So the two women, old friends from their media careers, attracted some seed capital from America Online, and took the plunge. They became internet entrepreneurs.

How iVillage evolved

iVillage was not the start. In fact, it is the culmination of several initiatives the duo have undertaken in developing their web business: 'Initially, we thought our venture would be aimed at the baby boomer age group and a generation that Nancy and I had been marketing to for a long time. We understood them intuitively, besides being them as well.'

photo © Helayne Seidman

That first initiative, and one that remains part of the iVillage tapestry, was Parent Soup, a site aimed at those raising children. This reflected the women's near-obsession with perfecting a product reflective of their audience and this is without doubt a crucial factor in the successful development of iVillage. However, one thing their experience of the media industry had taught them – with its love of ratings – was the value of market research and user feedback. 'It was about a year into the business that we found that disproportionately women, who made up just 8 percent of the web, flocked to iVillage,' says Carpenter. 'We thought this was interesting because this was the group that was probably getting the least from the internet.'

They dug deeper into the statistics. 'Women were starting businesses at twice the national average, women employed more people than the Fortune 500, women own more brokerage accounts,' recalls Carpenter. 'These were new developments emerging that hadn't really been noticed at the time we were looking at them. But they have certainly been noticed since,' she continues, with a nod towards the plethora of women's sites that have been launched in recent months.

'We realized that here was this phenomenon happening outside of the mainstream internet – but that the internet could actually be quite powerful in helping women manage these things in their lives.

'We felt that what had started as the Women's Movement was done, and now they were left with infinite opportunities and choices.'

Carpenter gives the example of women's magazines putting a glamorous figure on the front and expecting their readers to aspire to that image.

5 ways...

Candice
Carpenter
and Nancy
Evans broke
the rules

1   Their belief in a women-only site won them vital early funding.

2   Spotted the enormous potential in the female net market.

3   Pulled in advertisers that would not normally consider the net.

4   Put their users at the center of the business and built services around them.

5   Pioneered a unique management style where abilities suit the situation.

'It's not relevant to women's lives today,' she asserts. 'For example, Nancy's married with one child, I'm single with one child, and one adopted child, so already we have divergent paths. And if you multiply that out, there's already no consensus way to live your life.'

Thus the iVillage premise emerged. With women being offered more opportunities and choices than ever before, they were using this to transform the business market, the job market and the culture of the family. The internet could provide the perfect answer to helping women meet these new challenges and opportunities.

>> The internet could provide the perfect answer to helping
        women meet these new challenges and opportunities

Evans and Carpenter admit that iVillage emerged out of a 'process of elimination' following on from other roles they had experienced. Before iVillage, Evans created *Family Life* magazine, a move which topped 15 years in publishing. She was the winner of the 1989 Women in Communications Matrix Award for Excellence in Book Publishing.

Carpenter's managerial career began at American Express, where she held the position of vice-president of consumer marketing. Between 1989 and 1993, she was president of Time Life Video and Television, part of the Time Warner empire, where she oversaw the development of special interest and popular programming. Up until the founding of iVillage, Carpenter was also president of Q2, an upmarket shopping channel.

Evans says that even when they were part of these big organizations, 'We were both starting businesses within the organizations. Once you've done that, it's pretty hard to go back.'

iVillage's working culture

The notion of co-chairperson, joint chief executives, or however two founders split their roles, is a difficult one for most observers to contemplate, and iVillage is no different. After all, decisions have to be arrived at, rules have to be enforced and resolutions have to be made. Carpenter talks about trees, although the analogy escapes me. I think she is the root and branches to Evans's leaves. 'Nancy has an amazing sense of richness and detail and how to really bring something alive for the consumer,' she explains. 'I take the role of business architect.' Evans adds, 'We made a decision early on that we would not be in the same room at the same time unless we chose to because we wanted to divide and conquer and get going faster. We've changed our roles at different junctures depending on what was needed.'

Carpenter explains further:

'We probably haven't discussed this in more than a year because it's something we find so natural. It's more about trying to explain to other people what we find intuitively.

'I guess I work more in the abstract and Nancy makes it real. I actually think there are a lot of other ways of dividing up labor than in traditional hierachical companies where the size of your turf is equal to your value. That's just not true. The value of your contribution is equal to the value of the person.

'One of the most valuable people we have in the company has no one reporting to him. What we believe as a company is that you should find the thing that you are a 10 or 11 at and do that thing 24 hours a day.

'The point is to optimize who you are. Which actually tends to be a lot of fun because normally your job involves you utilizing a lot of strengths and your weaknesses so that you have to tend to drag yourself through the day.

'I think there are a lot of management issues that working for an internet company will change. People here tend to divide their jobs, which actually empowers them and helps them grow in their work. It has been a fascinating experience to go through, both culturally and organizationally.'

Evans agrees: 'It's important to underline that we would not have moved as fast as we did, or as we had to, if we hadn't been operating as dramatically a different structure as we did, as opposed to a traditional corporate culture.'

Was this an internet thing, or a female thing?

Carpenter, the more agitated and energetic of the two women, wrestles with the answer: 'I don't know because I'm part of both. In big companies, there's no choice in the way you work. Maybe it's a little bit of both – the people who have the biggest difficulty adjusting to our way of working are from bigger companies and are often male.'

This alternative management philosophy has permeated the development of the iVillage site. Evans gives an example:

'When we first launched Parent Soup, it was arranged by subject.

>> More than seven million women now
visit iVillage every month

'The structure for our home pages now is dramatically different: the door you choose to enter Parent Soup, for example, depends on the age of your child. This is a totally different way of getting to that issue than by subject.

'And that came from the feedback we got from users, rather than editors sitting in a room, coming up with ideas and assigning them.

'Thus the role of editor on our sites is not a conventional one – it's a listening one, listening to what the women are talking about in our chat rooms and on our message boards. That is pure market research and led us to where we are today.

'For example, when we saw that there were literally tens of thousands of women coming in to talk about fertility issues, we created an area just for them where their issues could be addressed.'

Evans points to another distinguishing feature of their sites:

'When women talk about things, they will talk about everything. They are global talkers. So that became iVillage – a place where women could go to to talk about their lives. Today, we have 17 sites on the things they care about. Women come to get things done, to get an answer to something. That's a real gender difference. Men want to surf, whereas women will bookmark three or four sites and keep coming back to them. That behavior has really been to our advantage.'

The result has been that more than seven million women now visit iVillage every month and the site ranks fourth for the length of time visitors spend there. Of those millions of visitors, one million are from outside the US. The potential for international expansion has not been lost on the two founders. Talks are already under way with partners in several overseas markets with a view to expanding the iVillage concept: 'iVillage as a model in helping women to solve things and get things done we think is something that will translate really well,' says Carpenter, adding that the notion of tailoring the content in response to what women want locally is another exportable winner.

Evans agrees: 'It's self-defining. Take the fertility example. We weren't doing that much on it, and our visitors came in, set up camp and we supported them. For that reason I think iVillage will travel as well to the UK as to Japan because the issues can be very different but the women will tell us what they are.'

Relationships with local service providers, or content creators, may be struck, but the sites will be branded iVillage. 'iVillage has a wonderful resonance in almost every culture,' says Carpenter. She adds, in her inimitable abstract way, 'In Japan, they're losing their towns and villages, so it's particularly resonant there.'

Future developments

Another development under discussion is the advent of broadband. Extra bandwidth will give community sites like iVillage greater capacity to provide interactive services and introduce additional offerings, such as video and audio. 'We don't subscribe to the notion that cable networks and internet brands are meant to be in some sort of marriage,' says Carpenter. 'But we do feel that as bandwidth becomes available there will be ways to use it in support of our position – helping women do things, choose things and make choices.' She continues:

'Most research shows that women use TV to recuperate. So it's not clear that putting something that women use as a tool on a medium they use to relax is going to work.

photo © Helayne Seidman

'What we are looking at are shorter versions. In other words, instead of assuming that television just moves to the internet, we're assuming television stays television and then on the internet you'll ultimately be able to use more voice, more video to support the same goals.'

Carpenter cites the example of recipes, which are already searchable and downloadable from iVillage, as something that could benefit from a two-minute video clip. 'But we're not going to add a half-hour cookery show because that's not the point.' The point is, she says, that visitors come to the site to get

1   Persuading visitors to spend more.

2   Increasing and improving e-commerce opportunities.

3   Building the iVillage brand against increasing competition.

4   Taking iVillage into other media.

5   Convincing investors of the iVillage business model.

5 hurdles...

for Candice Carpenter and Nancy Evans and iVillage

help and information quickly and succinctly – and the new video offerings will support that premise.

Such developments are important to iVillage as it seeks to exploit its undeniably strong position. However, its keenest challenge remains an ironic one: how to persuade women to stay on site and shop. Attracting women in as a resource is one thing, and the advertising revenues it brings in its wake are obviously welcome. But few doubt that those portals and community sites with the brightest future are those that can leverage their positions with regard to e-commerce. iVillage's showing in this area has been disappointing, although it has been pushing hard to improve matters.

The company's desire to increase e-commerce revenues has seen a flurry of end-of-year deals, including the $26 million acquisition of FamilyPoint.com, a photo gallery, address book and chat site. It also received $22.5m from PlanetRx for the drugs and vitamins group to sell its products via the iVillage site. Yet its share price is languishing. In a market where the appetite for net stocks remains ravenous, iVillage struggles to stay above its IPO price of March 1999.

The hard figures from the company's most recent results make typical reading for an internet company determined to spend its way to success. The question is whether, amid all the red ink, the building blocks to future revenue generation are being laid.

In its filing for its IPO, the company disclosed it had lost $76.3 million since its inception. In the nine months to September 1998, it achieved revenues of $9 million and made losses of $33 million. Its content, marketing and development costs amounted to $42.2 million. The company also warned, as it must, that 'Although our revenues have grown in recent quarters, we cannot assure you that we will achieve sufficient revenues for profitability.'

Marketing costs rose again in the third quarter of 1999, the group's most recent results, taking losses from $12.2 million to $28.4 million. Revenues jumped, however, from $4.29 million to $10.7 million. Advertising revenues continued to make up the bulk of the group's revenues.

Evans and Carpenter remain resolute in the face of their continuing losses and maintain that the group has a bright and independent future. 'Of course we've had plenty of approaches,' says Carpenter. But she says iVillage is very different to those community sites that have been snapped up by media companies:

>> There is little doubting iVillage's value as a web property.
Leveraging that value is the challenge for Carpenter and Evans

'Tripod and Geocities are what I'd call pure social community sites where people go for self-expression. We are much more of a demographic destination. In addition to a community, we have stores, personal shoppers, planning tools, experts – it's a very goal-directed place. I think that differentiates us quite a bit. They're about gathering – we're about gathering to get things done.

'The other thing is that those community sites did not monetize well when they were bought. iVillage has the highest revenue per user of any major internet site, which shows that we've been able to monetize it well. Our revenue per thousand page views is around $31, Yahoo is $5. Of course you'd expect a difference because we have a totally different business model. But even CNet is only at $26 and even the next women's site is at $17.

The power of community – how Ford learned to love women

Nancy Evans: The reason Ford came to iVillage as a major sponsor was not to sell cars – although that would have been an additional benefit. They came onto the site to become the car company that women liked, and they began by asking iVillage women what they wanted in a car.

Ford had suddenly realized that women are buying more cars than men, not just influencing the purchases, as they have done traditionally. And those figures eventually prevailed on their marketing wisdom.

Now what they have done is taken the ideas from literally thousands of our members and incorporated the top ones into a prototype car called the 'iVillager'.

Women are so wonderfully common sense. Ideas they suggested included:

- Seat belts designed not just for men – for us they either strangle us up here or cut across less than desirable places. So now they're going to be fitting seat belts to suit women as well.

- Accelerator pedals wreck women's high heels, so they're changing the way the accelerator operates.

- Cup holders everywhere in the car so that kids and not just the driver have somewhere – I mean this is all so basic.

- And make those containers flexible so they hold different sized drinks.

- What about little tray tables that come down off the back seat so that kids can use them for drawing?

- How about another mirror next to the driver's one so that I can look up and see my kids in the back without having to turn round and cause an accident?

- And when you go grocery shopping and you put the bags in the boot and they all fall over – how about having dividers so the bags stand up?

It was the most beautiful thing, and the replies are still coming in. Now how valuable a thing was that for Ford? They got all this fabulous research from real women, and women got to change the way cars are.

> **Candice Carpenter:** People loving your brands is as important as knowing your brands.
>
> **Nancy Evans:** And there is no more powerful medium than the internet for making that happen.

'So this combination of community, intentionality, problem solving and women is very powerful economically. Those other community sites almost had to be bought because they hadn't geared up totally to their business model. They got enormous amounts of traffic but hadn't balanced it up as to how you monetize it as a business. They were born to be adjuncts of something else, whereas iVillage wasn't.'

There is little doubting iVillage's value as a web property. Leveraging that value is the challenge for Carpenter and Evans. Would the company be better off sitting under the wing of one of the big portals, such as Yahoo or MSN, and receiving the traffic – and revenues – that would generate? Or perhaps sitting with a deep-pocketed traditional media company?

The two entrepreneurs would argue that it has been their independence from such organizations that has allowed them to develop the business the way they have; returning to the big company confines, particularly in the latter case, would stifle their corporate creativity.

But there remains a sense that iVillage's expenditure, and the length of time it must continue to bear that load, will at some stage require it to seek help. A merger with other women's sites might be one way forward. Certainly the flood of IPOs at the end of 1999 suggests that the market for multi-brands in the women's market is as strong on the internet as it is in the traditional media market of magazines.

As the biggest in the sector, iVillage would certainly approach any consolidation in a strong position. Whatever the outcome, the energy and drive of Candice Carpenter and the operational expertise of Nancy Evans are likely to ensure that the two entrepreneurs' roles are undiminished.

❝ I am one of the voices that reminds us where we came from, reminds us of our responsibilities **❞**

12

Pierre Omidyar
eBay

Bidding to distance the competition

I am the founder and the chairman so I primarily keep my role focussed on our vision, thinking about where we are going to be heading for the next couple of years.

I give Meg some counsel on occasion and I work on various issues that kind of interest me with regards to the community with different teams. They are addressing those throughout eBay so I am kind of one of the voices. We have several in the company but I am one of the voices that reminds us where we came from, reminds us of our responsibilities.

Introduction

Think eBay, think Meg Whitman. The vivacious CEO of the internet's biggest auction company has been the primary focus for investors and observers alike as eBay has stolen a march on its rivals.

Yet behind Whitman stands the founder and chairman of the company, the softly spoken Pierre Omidyar. It is Omidyar who invented the eBay concept and has continued to lay the strategy for the company's success. Indeed, he has recently relocated to Paris from California to lead the company's charge into Europe.

The formation of eBay

The success of eBay owes much to its capturing of the pioneering spirit of the internet – bringing people together in a way unimaginable before the medium's invention. However, the idea of a global community of people swapping and of auctioning their unwanted goods came from a combination of the straightforward and the bizarre.

It was 1995, and the young Omidyar, a technical graduate, was becoming disenchanted with the growing commercialization of the internet. At the same time, he was also searching for a special present for his girlfriend, who was a collector of sorts. He takes up the story:

'My wife, who was my fiancée at the time, was a collector of these Pez candy dispensers. They come with heads of different cartoon characters, and they also have seasonal characters and so forth, so they are collectible.

5 ways...

Pierre
Omidyar
broke the
rules

1 Uniquely recognized that the internet was about individuals and not the corporate opportunity.

2 Brought auctions to the web in a way that immediately appealed and worked commercially.

3 Never got too enamored by technology and so never lost sight of the core objectives of the company.

4 Delegated control by bringing in experienced management in the form of Meg Whitman.

5 Has never stood still and has taken the eBay brand forward into other forms of auction.

'And we had been talking about how difficult it was to find other people who collected these particular items, so that was one thing that was going through my mind at that time back in 1995.

'The other thing was I was really interested in doing something on the web that would bring the power of the internet to individual people, as opposed to big companies.

'There were a lot of commercial efforts going on in the web in 1995, but they were all really focussed on how do I sell more things to more people and increase corporate sales and all that. The web had grown up very much an individual and democratic thing... and what I wanted to do was bring the web to benefit individuals.'

These two concerns – the difficulties facing the collector and the growing exploitation of the web – were explored by Omidyar within the context of his fascination with the mechanics of the marketplace: 'I had always been interested in financial markets and the whole concept of their efficiency. In an efficient market goods would reach their correct market price.'

There was also his technology background to bring to the feast:

'I started off as a software engineer, with my computer science degree. I was really interested in developing different technology for consumer products. I loved the idea of being able to take a concept all the way through to delivering to the consumers, seeing their reactions and then actually modifying it.

'And the internet gives you the best place to do that, because you can publish software instantly, you can get reactions from your customers instantly, you know if you did something wrong straight away.

'So, I kind of took all those things together and as a hobby in my spare time, I put together the first website in 1995 to let people auction off their items. That's how the thing got started.'

This was not Omidyar's first stab at a start-up. In 1991, he had founded eSharp with some friends, a venture that was eventually sold to Microsoft. However, the experience did not leave him enamored with being an entrepreneur. 'Before eBay, I never wanted to run a company,' he admits. 'In fact, I wanted to avoid it.'

In moving to Paris, Omidyar is returning to the city where he was born and which his family left to move to the US when he was six. It is an experience, he believes, that has shaped his thinking:

'I have been more, I guess, observational in nature because I came from outside of the US. I do like to observe and learn from different systems – and how the markets work. And markets are based on people, so getting an understanding of how people work and how people can interact to create an efficient market is something I have always had an interest in.'

It was fairly early on after he had built the site that Omidyar realized he had hit on something big:

'I knew it was a useful service in the early days because people were coming on, using it, and paying for it.

'It was rather surprising that the business was actually making money – but the rapid pace at which people kind of grabbed on to it and started using it to pursue their passions and collecting, that was really surprising.'

Rapid growth for eBay

The enthusiastic response from web users presented difficult managerial and technical challenges for the young company.

'From an organizational perspective it was very difficult,' recalls Omidyar. 'We grew very, very rapidly in terms of employees, and after the IPO of September 1998 we grew even faster.

'Then there were the acquisitions - we bought a few companies, and integrating them into the core operations is always a challenge for a company. But when you do it in an environment where your core business is growing, say, 10 percent a month or something like that, it's pretty phenomenal, it is challenging.'

Omidyar and his first employee Jeff Skoll, turned to Meg Whitman, a former senior executive with Hambro and Disney, to become CEO and take over the operational side of the business:

'Jeff and I always believe in bringing people on board who are smarter than us, and who know how to do things better than us. I knew from the beginning that I would need to bring on another CEO to replace me if we were going to build a public company.

'I really wanted someone who had a lot more experience than I did in terms of consumer branding, marketing and actually running a large organization. Meg brought both sides of the consumer marketing and the general management in one person and has been a phenomenal addition.'

Phenomenal indeed. By the end of 1999, eBay was the most visited e-commerce site on the internet, surpassing the mighty Amazon. According to figures from net research house Media Metrix, eBay drew in more than one million daily visitors in the last week of November 1999.

In its latest results, net income more than trebled to $1.35 million in the third quarter 1999, with sales increasing likewise to $58.5 million. While the results pleased analysts, there was disappointment that eBay warned that it would increase marketing expenditure substantially to head off fierce competition, particularly from the big portal groups. Meanwhile, the figures showed the number of registered users at the eBay site increased fromm 5.6 million to 7.7 million in the previous quarter and up from 1.3 million in the same period a year ago. The value of all goods sold on the site jumped from $195 million to $741 million year-on-year. Analysts estimate eBay's share of the on-line auction market at around 90 percent. Little surprise that its shares have risen 25-fold since going public.

>> By the end of 1999, eBay was the most visited
e-commerce site, surpassing the mighty Amazon

From consumer collectibles, eBay has added an impressive list of product categories to its marketplace as the business has grown. Omidyar says this is only part of where the company can go:

'Our vision is building a global marketplace where people can trade practically anything on earth, and the global part of that is really just beginning.

'We already operate the largest site in Europe which is eBay Germany, and we've just launched eBay UK. Europe is growing very rapidly from an internet perspective so we see a lot of growth ahead of us in the core business.'

Expansion here may be by a variety of routes:

'We really can enter countries in multiple ways. If we see a player in the country that seems to really understand it, understand the market and what it takes to make a good job, we would like to acquire them. That happened with Orlando in Germany which we acquired back in June and they are doing great and running ebay Germany.'

This expansion involves considerable start-up costs. The business of collectibles is both labor- and time-intensive, involving the creation of a community of like-minded individuals in order to kick-start the market. Added to this is the fact that the internet market in general and the auction market in particular have changed substantially since the days when eBay was establishing itself in the US. Competition, for example, is intense with some of the biggest players in the internet space now offering an auction service. Indeed auctions have become almost *de rigueur* for any self-respecting portal site.

Overseas competition, likewise, will be met with the same eBay strategy:

'For example, in the UK, we are trying to grow the business the same way we did in the US and that's from the grass roots. It requires a lot of manpower because we are going to trade shows and meeting with collectors there, building relationships with other communities. It's something that requires a lot of people and a lot of sensitivity to those needs.'

It is this sensitivity Omidyar believes is important as it enables eBay to respond to the needs of the local market:

'We want to make sure we are addressing the most important markets first and we want to make sure that we do those well.'

'Everything we learn in one market we can apply to the next market. This isn't as simple as duplicating what we did in the US and doing it here – every European market is different, with different cultural backgrounds, different historical values, and so it will require different approaches.'

Expansion in the domestic market is also being undertaken with the launch of regional auction sites. Omidyar explains:

'What we discovered was that while eBay was a really neat way to trade things that you could shoot back and forth, people also decided to start putting on certain types of merchandise that's not as easy to shift.

1 Policing against items of bad taste, which threaten the company's reputation.

2 Guarding against growing competition, particularly from Amazon and Yahoo.

3 Building on the vertical opportunity with more acquisitions of allied bricks and mortar operations.

4 Building partnerships with on-line financial services companies in order to extend the means through which eBay customers can transact with each other.

5 Not becoming complacent about the domestic US market while expanding abroad.

5 hurdles... for Pierre Omidyar and eBay

'These were things that you would actually want to inspect before trading. So in a regional marketplace you tend to see more what we call practical and premium-type goods – like golf clubs or washing machines, or a sofa, to premium items like automobiles or pianos.'

In December 1999, the company launched 23 regional websites. It also signed an alliance with Athlete Direct to enable users to bid on sports equipment from local sports stars.

Challenges and potential problems

Competition for eBay has come from both ends of the internet spectrum, from start-ups to the biggest names on the web. Omidyar believes eBay's first-to-market advantage, critical mass and focus on creating vibrant marketplaces, gives it a significant edge over its rivals:

'It's important to remember that the business we are in is creating marketplaces. We bring buyers and sellers together to exchange goods – and if you are a buyer you are looking for the largest selection.

'Likewise, if you are a seller you're looking at where to sell your item and how much you will get for it. In both cases, it's basically about the largest marketplace. And in the US, it's eBay.

'Sure, it's been very difficult – we have seen a lot of competitors come in, some of whom have been better capitalized than us. But it's difficult for them to create a new service that draws people away from eBay because that existing market is already there.

'Our two key competitors in the US are Yahoo and Amazon. Yet they represent a very, very small portion of the total business that goes on in the United States person to person.'

Omidyar underlines the eBay advantage:

'It's primarily the fact that there is a vibrant and effective marketplace at work. It's like a network effect, so the idea is that if you are going to buy a fax machine you want to make sure your fax machine can communicate with everybody else's fax machine. So if there are different formats then that would be silly.

'It's the same as the VHS versus Beta battle – although Beta was a better format, VHS proliferated more quickly. So although the consumer could have bought a better format, they decided to buy a format that was more compatible with everyone else's so they could be part of that network. It's a virtuous cycle that occurs – you bring buyers on that attract sellers and you bring sellers on that attract buyers and it goes into a virtuous cycle that keeps feeding on itself.'

Does he fear any of the competition?

'Well we do keep a good eye on our competitors. We try to learn from what they are doing and the fact that the two in the US are probably the two best internet companies out there is in some ways a compliment.'

'What sets us apart is that we are singularly focussed on helping individuals do business with one another and that's all we do.

'We don't care about selling books, music, or dog food or whatever it is. That I think is one of our key successes in the US and I hope will be in Europe as well.'

The consistent problems to have faced the company have been moral and technical ones. In the former category, eBay has been criticized for having people auctioning human organs, Nazi memorabilia and live rare animals. Omidyar takes a phlegmatic stance:

'Well, eBay is an open marketplace. Not only is it a large vibrant marketplace but every day we get anywhere from 300 000 to 400 000 new listings. Every single day there are 3 million listings, so you are bound to get some people putting up some strange things. However, eBay doesn't actually sell anything, so we were never doing anything wrong or offering any kind of illegal goods.

'What happens sometimes is either sellers don't know any better or they are pranksters who come on the service and our community has always been good at spotting these people, letting us know about them so that we can take appropriate action.

'It's always going to be a part of any kind of marketplace. Like a city will always have a certain part of it that's not ideal but well over 99.99 percent of our transactions happen without a hitch and that's really the magic of eBay.'

Indeed, the eBay magic worked for its founder and chairman early on:

'I bought a laser pointer and these are the little red dots for presentation but they are also cat toys. I don't know if you have every played with them with a cat – that's really what they are for, not presentations – you chase the dot around the floor, on the wall and the cats just run after it, it's wonderful.

'So after about two weeks of that the cat was still going but the laser point was not. It had stopped working. I replaced the battery but it didn't start working again so I decided I would throw the thing away. Then I thought, why not put it up on eBay and see what happens? So I listed it on the site as a broken laser pointer, I described it and said I'd replaced the battery and it still didn't work, I'd paid $30 for it, so start bidding at $1.

'By the end of the two-week auction, the laser sold for $14 – almost half of what I paid for it – to somebody who is quite happy and plans to take it apart. I think that's when I realized one man's trash is another man's treasure and really turning something I was going to throw away into $14 hard cash was kind of cool.'

However, the founder and chairman is not a collector:

'People do ask me if I am a collector, but I'm not, though I enjoy learning about other people's collections. I get quite excited about them and I will go on eBay to see if I can find some interesting things. I also spend some time thinking about complexity theory and how networks systems interact. eBay is a perfect example of an organic system that has evolved into a complex adaptable system and that's kind of neat.'

The company's most glamorous acquisition to date has been that of Butterfield & Butterfield, the auspicious San Franciscan auction house. Omidyar explains:

'The acquisition has gone very well. They are the only traditional auctioneers – and we have talked to all the big ones – who really seem to understand what the internet is about.

>> Omidyar is determined to keep eBay's focus on its
   service, rather than what the latest technology can do

'We intend to use them to gain some more knowledge about fine arts, decorative collectibles and to launch our eBay great collections product. It's enabling us to bring this high-quality authenticated and guaranteed merchandise from dealers across the world.'

It is the kind of detail the company prides itself on and underlines the management's belief in itself as an auction company first and an internet group second. In fact, Omidyar is determined to keep eBay's focus on its service, rather than what the latest technology can do:

'One of the interesting things about eBay is that we have always lagged behind internet technology. We make very little use of Java these days even though it's been around for a long time and that's primarily because our customers have also. They use all sorts of browsers and have old computers and slower modems and all that kind of thing. Unlike some internet companies, we're very agnostic about technology.'

This may strike some observers as odd, given the technical problems that have beset the company. Its latest results revealed the company had been forced to spend almost $9 million on a new back-up computer system, as well as increasing its technical staff by 50 percent. The company has been plagued by 'outages', the term used when a site collapses. An outage in June 1999 kept the site closed for 22 hours and sent the eBay share price tumbling. With competitors circling, the additional systems expenditure was warmly applauded by Wall Street.

Looking to the future

Technical problems and the odd liver for sale aside, eBay's rise has seemed unstoppable. By creating a unique marketplace with mass appeal – who doesn't after all have a cupboard full of unwanted or unused items – the company has established itself as the leading e-commerce site on the web. And tapping the huge and ill-served market for collectibles has only underscored its popularity.

Even the advent of the likes of Microsoft, Excite and Lycos into the auction market has left little or no trace on eBay's inexorable growth. Meanwhile, the group, through the co-axis of Omidyar and Whitman, has not rested on its laurels. New services, product categories and partners have only served to strengthen eBay's position.

So what challenges does the company now face? Managing its growth will be key. With senior staff, such as Omidyar, focussed on overseas expansion, the domestic market must not be neglected. While initiatives such as the regional auction sites are innovative, the company needs to take a more proactive attitude towards technology and the developments on the horizon to stay further ahead of the market. For example, the advent of digital television with internet access would seem to hold a certain attraction for a mass market business like eBay. Yet Omidyar says the company will adopt a wait-and-see policy in relation to the new medium.

One can hardly blame him. The company's roaring success has been built around a simple idea and the available technology. And such is the group's commanding lead, he can afford to be relaxed in the face of the chasing pack: 'We are building a global brand and a global business here. We are giving the power of commerce back to the individual.'

Index

Abaca 122
Abacus 16
AC Neilson 90
acquisitions/partnerships by
AltaVista 137, 139–40
Amazon 72–5, 76
E*Trade 95
eBay 182, 185, 188
iVillage 171
Lycos 5, 10–12, 12–14
Yahoo! 12, 29, 31–3
advertising expenditure 82
Affiliate Network 131, 138
airline industry 41–2, 45
Alamo 47
Allen, Paul 46
alliances *see* acquisitions/partnerships
AltaVista 15, 126–40
acquisitions 137
Affiliate Network 131, 138
business strategy 131, 134–8
capital investment in 138
CMGI ownership 136
e-commerce initiatives 137
future partnerships 139–40
international expansion 1 38
proposed IPO 140
workforce 137

Amazon 64–77
acquisitions strategy 76
auction site 75
customer service ratings 75
electronics and software
business 75
expansion plans 75–7
formation 68–70
mission 71
music site 72
partnerships 72–5
revenues 76–7
toy store 74
z-shops 13, 71
America Online (AOL) 13, 21, 129
Netscape takeover 61–2
America West 42, 44
American Airlines 44
American Express 81, 166
Ameritrade Holdings 81
Andreesen, Marc 57
Angelfire 12
AOL *see* America Online (AOL)
Ashford.com 74
AT&T 53, 56–7, 159
@Home 157–9
Athlete Direct 185
auction sites 28, 75, 184

Audible.com 75
AutoNation 47

Back to Basics Toys 74
Barksdale Group 62
Barksdale, Jim xvii, 50–63, 90–1
    breaking the rules 58
    at Federal Express 56
    at IBM 54
    joining Netscape 53–7
    at McCaw Cellular 56–7
    Microsoft job offer 53, 57
    political interests 63
Bell, George 155–7, 159
Benchmark Capital 57
Bertlesmann 13
Bezos, Jeff xvi, xxii, 64–77
    breaking the rules 70
    hurdles 73
Braddock, Richard 43
branding strategies xviii, 8–9
broadcast.com 29
Budget 47
budgeting systems 60
Burn Rate 99
burn rates xxi
business strategy
    AltaVista 131, 134–8
    Lycos 8–10
    Yahoo 24–9
Butterfield & Butterfield 16, 188
Byrne, David 57

cable companies xix
Cambex 7
car rental services 47

Carpenter, Candice xvi, 160–74
    at American Express 166
    breaking the rules 166
    hurdles 171
    at Q2 167
    at Time Warner 166–7
cellular phone groups xix
certified delivery services 104–5
Chambers, John 63
Clarke, Jim 57
Clinton, Bill 110–11
CMGI 15, 136, 139–40
CNet 172
Comcast 159
Commtouch 103
community sites 172
Compaq Computer 132–3
Condé Nast 72
Continental Airlines 44
control xxiii–xxiv
Cook Industries 56
Cotsakos, Christos xvii, 78–95, 107–9
    background 81, 82–7
    breaking the rules 84
    at Federal Express 88–90
    hurdles 89
    joining E*Trade 81, 90–1
    motivation 92–3
    in Vietnam 85–7
Cox Communications 159
Critical Path 96–111
    and E*Trade 107–9
    formation 104–6
    initial challenges 106–7
cryptography 39
culture

at Excite 156
at iVillage 167–70
at Yahoo! 30–1
Currie, Peter 62
customer satisfaction xxiii

Davis, Bob xvi, 1–16, 139
    breaking the rules 6
    business roots 7
    hurdles 11
    joining Lycos 5–8
Dell, Michael 63
Delta 44–6
Democratic Party website 109–11
Digital Equipment 132
Diller, Barry 3
Disney 115–16, 117, 120
Dore, John 57
Double Click 16
drugstore.com 72–3

E*Trade 78–95
    advertising expenditure 82
    and Critical Path 107–9
    future plans 93–5
    partnerships 95
    revenues 82
    Softbank investment in 91–2
eBay xxii, 16, 176–90
    acquisitions/alliances 182, 185, 188
    competitors 185–6
    criticisms of 187
    formation 179–82
    future challenges 189–90
    growth of 182–5
    international expansion 183–4
    new listings 187

regional websites 184–5
    revenues 183
    technical problems 189
    visitors to the site 182–3
entrepreneurial qualities 55
eSharp 181
Evans, Nancy xvi, 160–74
    breaking the rules 166
    Family Life magazine 166
    hurdles 171
Excite xxi, xxiv, 104, 143–59
    @Home merger 157–9
    culture 156
    formation of 148–9
    revenues 158
    start-up finance 152–5
Excite (*cont.*)
    tracking stock plans 159
Expedia 37

Family Life 166
FamilyPoint.com 171
Federal Express 56, 88–90, 108
Fidelity Investments 13
Filo, David 21, 22–3, 30
First Auction 14
Ford 173–4
Frame Technology 118

Gamesville.com 12
Gates, Bill 37, 53, 58
GeoCities 12, 172
Go 115–17, 131
Greenlight.com 74

Hayden, David xvii, xxi–xxii, 96–111
    breaking the rules 100

Hayden, David (*cont.*)
  and the Democratic Party website
    109–11
  formation of Critical Path 104–6
  hurdles 105
  property development company
    100, 101
  Wolff New Media/Magellan deal
    103–4
Highland Capital 5
horizontal portals 71–2
HotBot 12

I-Atlas 137
IBM 12, 54, 132
ideas xx–xxii
incubator funds 109
Infoseek 112–25
  formation 117–21
  Go.com link 115–17
  recruitment problems 116
Internet Shopping Network 14
iVillage xxiii, 160–74
  acquisitions 171
  culture 167–70
  Ford sponsorship 173–4
  future developments 170–4
  international expansion 169–70
  revenues 171–2

Jermoluk, Tom 159
Johnson, Robin 116

Khosla, Vinod 153
Kirsch, Steve xvii, 112–25
  early career 117–18
  electric vehicle campaign 123

formation of Abaca/Propel.com 122
formation of Infoseek 118–21
Foundation website 124
future plans 121–5
sale of Infoseek 120
Kleiner Perkins 153, 155
Koogle, Tim 19, 30

Kraus, Joe xvii, 143–59
  breaking the rules 148
  hurdles 155
  microfiche duplicating job 147
  role in Excite 150–2
  T-shirt design company 146, 147–8

Lane, Ray 63
laser pointers 187–8
Living.com 74–5
Lotus 12
Lutch, Ben 145
Lycos 1–16
  acquisitions and alliances 5, 10–12
  and AltaVista 139–40
  business strategy 8–10
  initial public offering 11–12
  international expansion 13–14
  mission 1
  partnership strategy 12–14
  takeover of 16
  USA Networks merger 3–4, 14–16
  working capital 11
LYCOshop 13

McCaw Cellular 53, 56–7
McCue, Mike 62
McIntyre, Ryan 145
McKinley 102
Magellan 99, 102–4

MailCity 12
Mallett, Jeff 19, 22, 30
market share xviii
Maxwell, Christine 101
Maxwell, Isabel 99, 101, 103
Merrill Lynch 81
Microsoft 53, 57
    Expedia travel business 37
    Priceline law suit 40
Morgan Stanley 81, 139
Mouse Systems 118
MSN 129
MyTime.com 12

Net2Phone 47
Netscape xxii, 50–63
    America Online (AOL) takeover of
        61–2
    budgeting system 60
    revenue growth 58–60
Northwest Airlines 44, 46
Nova, Dan 5

Omidyar, Pierre xvi–xvii, xxiv, 176–90
    breaking the rules 180
    early career 181
    eSharp formation 181
    hurdles 185

Packard Bell 12
Parent Soup 165, 168
partnerships *see*
        acquisitions/partnerships
Partovi, Hadi 62
patents 37, 39–40, 46
Perfect YardSale 48
Perot, Ross 54

Pfeifer, Eckhard 134
PlanetRX 171
portal model 130
Porter, Bill 81, 90–1
Priceline 34–9
    business concept 41–3
    Delta agreement 44–6
    financial viability 37, 43
    formation 38–41
    initial public offering (IPO) 46
    latest initiatives 46–9
    launch 43
    patents 37, 39–40, 46
    Perfect YardSale 48
    revenues 47–8
profits *see* revenues/profits
Propel.com 122

Q2 167

RagingBull.com 137
recruitment problems 116
Research on Demand 101, 102
revenues/profits xv, xviii–xix
    Amazon 76–7
    E*Trade 82
    eBay 183
    Excite 158
    iVillage 171–2
    Netscape 58–60
    Priceline 47–8
    Yahoo! 21
Rheinfeld, Martin 145
Rosen, Ben 134

Schrock, Rod xvi, 126–40
    breaking the rules 130

Schrock, Rod (*cont.*)
   business career 132–3
   childhood 131–2
   hurdles 135
   joining AltaVista 129, 133–4
Schulman, Daniel 48
Shatner, William xx, 42–3
shopping.com 137
Skoll, Jeff 182
Smith, Fred 56, 89–90, 108
Smith, Quincy 62
Softbank 91–2
Sonique 12
Soros, George 46
sothebys.amazon.com 75
Spencer, Graham 145, 154
Stanford University 145–6
start-up businesses 55
strategy *see* business strategy
Sun Microsystems 61
Supercard 149

TD Waterhouse 81
TechNet 63
Tellme Networks 62
Terra Networks 16
Terry's Guide To The World Wide
   Web 23
Ticketmaster 14, 15
Time Warner 21, 166–7
Tripod 12, 172
TWA 42, 44

United Airlines 44
US Airways 41, 44
USA Networks 3–4, 14–16
VanHaren, Mark 145
venture capital 6, 55, 108–9, 152–5

vertical portals 71–2
Walker Digital 37, 38, 39, 48
Walker, Jay xvii, xx, 34–49
   background 38
   breaking the rules 40
   hurdles 45
Wang 7
Warehouse Club 46
WebMD 13
Wetherall, David 15, 136, 140
Whitman, Meg 179, 182
WhoWhere 12
Wingspan.com 13
Wired News 12
Wolff, Michael 99, 103–4

Yahoo! xxiii, 18–33, 129, 134, 135
   acquisitions 12, 29
   advertising model 27
   auctions 28
   business strategy 24–9
   business-to-business model 29
   business-to-consumer model 28
   culture 30–1
   formation 22–4
   international expansion 32–3
   page views 21
   partnerships 31–3
   revenues 21
   shopping section 28
   travel 28
Yang, Jerry xvi, xxiii, xxiv, 18–33
   background 22
   breaking the rules 26
   formation of Yahoo! 22–4
   hurdles 29

z-shops 13, 71
Zip2 137